Roberto Bettini

Wherever there is great cycling, they are there, with a third eye that's their camera, shooting photos with the sensitivity of one who loves the sport of cycling and who understand the inside secrets of the sport. Roberto Bettini and Graham Watson are among the most popular photographers on the international cycling circuit. And they are also good friends. Once their work finishes at the Tour de France or at the World Cup Classics, often at the end of a long, tough day, they often find themselves together in front of a beer or a glass of good red wine. And all the top riders know them and appreciate their professionalism. So from the meetings of these two friends comes the photographic memory of cycling and thus, the book of the year in cycling is born. Thanks to the hundred of splendid images, the story of the great moments of the season is told. It's a unique documentation that shows what happened in the world of two wheels.

Graham Watson

The images of Roberto Bettini and Graham Watson manage to astound us every year. And to help us re-live the infinite emotions of a long, intense racing season. Their understanding and their lenses bring us up close and personal with the great champions, at the most crucial moments on the roads of the most important races.

For the 11th time, they have launched this special editorial initiative, that the UCI is particularly lease to support; a book that as you turn it's pages, will serve as an extraordinary way to jog you memory.

Cycling is a totally unique sport. Also because we have the privilege to offer you, on time, phot creations from Roberto Bettini, Graham Watson and their collaborators.

As well, on eve of the era of the ProTour, this edition of 2004 has a special historic value, with the story fo the final races of the World Cup Series.

One more reason that each and every passionate cycling enthusiast should find a special place for this book in their own library.

Hein Verbruggen
President UCI

Paolo Bettini

The old pro, the new kid and many confirmations.

Lance Armstrong, at almost 33 years old, won his sixth consecutive Tour De France and entered in to the history books. Damiano Cunego, almost 23 years old, emerged at the Giro d'Italia and closed his season with a classy performance at Lombardia. 20 years after Hinault, Cunego won in Como and cycling has discovered a new champion who can win both grand tours and the one day monuments of cycling. To realize the impact of Cunego's performance, all you have to do is to remember that the last rider to win the Giro and Lombardia in the same season was Eddy Merckx and only legends like Coppi, Bartali, Guerra, Binda and Girardengo have don it before.

Armstrong and Cunego are the cover boys of this book, which provides the beautiful moments of cycling in 2004. Paolo Bettini is also here; Olympic gold medalist and winner of the World Cup for the third consecutive year, and Oscar Freire, World Champion for the third time, once again in Verona where he won in 1999. Speaking of hat-tricks, Roberto Heras won his third Vuelta, which only the Swiss rider Tony Rominger had done before. Another hat-trick was that of Davide Rebellin, the only man in cycling history to win Amstel Gold Race, Fleche Wallone and Liege-Bastogne-Liege all in one week. Alessandro Petacchi showed he's Number One sprinter (9 stages at the Giro and 4 at the Vuelta), while Ivan Basso and Andreas Kloden both continued to improve in the big races.

But any technical analysis of the season should start with the memory of Marco Pantani. Yes, because 2004, before being remebered as the year of Armstrong e Cunego, will be remembered as the year of the tragedy of Pantani. Il Pirata was always an original champion; a man outside the usual parameters. Unable to live a normal life and needing to live on the limits, Marco Pantani finally ended up in free fall.

We knew later he had personal issues (cocaine) and we knew later he was trying to get out of the black hole of depression, but no one expected such a tragic end for him. His last race was the 2003 Giro d'Italia 2003, where he finished in 14th place overall. Marco died about 5am on Saturday February 14th. He died on St. Valentine's Day, in an anonymous apartment in Rimini. He was dead after slowly giving up everything:
cycling, his family, his friends....

Afterwards, his autopsy showed he died of a cocaine overdose, just a sad confirmation of his problems, so hurtful that made him finally fall so far. He died without asking for help, he died alone and his long silence will remain the most powerful scream of the year.

Cycling has lost something with the absence of Pantani, but as they say in show business, the show must go on. And perhaps it was a sign of destiny that the talent of Cunego first showed itself, who was inspired by il Pirata. Starting as Simoni's key support rider, Cunego took advantage of the first opportunity to be in front. Without betraying his captain,pushed by the enthusiasm of the fans, Cunego conquered the Maglia Rosa and managed the situation well after he showed he was the best rider in the mountains.

No real story in the Tour of Armstrong. Lance, in comparision to his adversaries, was stronger than ever. He won like the Cannible, even going after stage wins. Like Merckx. His sixth consecutive Yellow Jersey is one of the most intense chapters in the story of sports. Armstrong continued to be an example of sheer determination besides his mastery of race tactics. He continues to carry with him on his bicycle his message of hope and cancer survivorship. And this is what characterizes and makes unique his champions personality.

Too bad that Lance threw in the sponge right after the Tour. An Olympic time trial title could have been his, a World Championship in Verona or a major classic would have given more depth to his achievements of July. The risk is that the strongest rider in the world will be remembered only as the greatest specialist of the Tour. Lance can do it because his success at the Tour is worth more (in media and economic terms) than the rest of the season. But cycling is the loser when it misses what a personality like Armstrong could and should offer.

Another great example of dedication and quality is Paolo Bettini. The Cricket confirmed he was number one in single day races, dominating the Athens Olympics and battling for his third consecutive World Cup after fighting until the end, until the last climbs of Lombardia, with Davide Rebellin.

Oscar Freire, a cool winner of Milano-Sanremo, is ready when the World Championship jersey is up for grabs. The organizers at Verona shortened the course (with two extra laps of the Torricelle climb) to make the race harder, but the result was the same as 1999. So Freire was there no matter what. He was an unknown and anticipated the others on the final straightaway, but this time he was one of the favorites and had a big win ahead of Erik Zabel and Luca Paolini.

Erik Zabel lost, by being too sure of himself, Milano-Sanremo, as well as being beaten at the Worlds. But to him nonetheless goes the Oscar of Work, because from February to October, he was a protagonist of all the sprints that count and finishes the season in third place in the world ranking behind Cunego and Bettini.

In the call to action this season, above all Jan Ullrich and Mario Cipollini were missed. For the Kaiser, his win in the Tour of Switzerland and fourth place at the Tour wasn't enough. The Lion King, on the other hand, was unlucky. Hi crash in the Giro d'Italia compromised his comeback at the Tour. Mario will race again, for at least another year, to end his career like Cipollini and not in his own shadow. And Johan Museeuw nor Richard Virenque won't be at the races anymore, two of the major stars of the 1990's.
Museeuw retired in the spring, while Virenque finshed the season after having won a nice stage in
<his> Tour de France.

From the tragedy of Pantani to the sprint of Cunego along Lake Como, cycling continues to offer an extraordinarily intense history. 2005 should begin with a new sign, the Pro Tour, but it will always be the riders, and their challenges that provide substance to our emotions beyond any name change or reorganization of the race calendar.

Pier Bergonzi

Oscar

Camels & Rugs: it's the Tour of Qatar. First sprint of the season to spanish rider Francisco Ventoso. Two stages and final gc to Robert Hunter.

Tour Down Under

The sumer sun shines in Australia. At the end of January, in the Tour Down Under, wins the experienced Patrick Jonker.

Tour de Langkawi

In Malaysia, the other start to the season. Smiling Colombian Freddy Gonzalez was the winner.

Paris-Nice

Jorg Jolssche

Alexandre Vinokourov

Tirreno-Adriatico

The revelation of Parigi-Nice was German Jorg Jaksche

Oscar Freire

At Tirreno-Adriatico, Paolo Bettini shined

95ªMilano Sanremo

Erik Zabel though he had it. The German raised his hands to the sky at the finish line and is passed, thanks to his perfect bike throw, by Oscar Freire. Only fourth was the big favorite Alessandro Petacchi.

Oscar Freire

Protagonists of <La Classicissima>. Left, Ludo Dierckxsens. Center, Paolo Bettini follows Yaroslav Popovych. The determination of Celestino. Right, an attack along the Riviera.

Semana Catalana

Levi Leipheiner

Beat Zberg

Criterium International

German rider Voigt dominated Criterium International. Armstrong was third

88ªRonde van Vlaanderen

The Campaign of the North took off with German Steffan Wasemann who won the Tour Of Flanders, second race of the World Cup between Bruges and Meerbeke.

Johan Museeuw says goodbye to <his> race.
The Flemish rider, numero uno rider in one day
races of his generation is the symbol of Flanders.

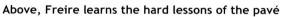
Above, Freire learns the hard lessons of the pavé

Roberto Petito

Benoit Joachim

Moments from Tour Of Flanders Below:
the mythical climb of Grammont

The first time a Swedish rider wins the Queen Of The Classics. Magnus Backsted, the gigantic Viking, wins Parigi-Roubaix.

Below, the determination of Backstedt, as he rides through a difficult pavé section.

Part of the Arenberg Forest, key point in Paris-Roubaix. At right, one of the first of pavé in the campaign of the North.

PAVÉS DU
PARIS-ROUBAIX

Commune de Bersée
Pavé du Nouveau Monde

Pays de Pévèle
Communauté de Communes

1780
mètres

Backstedt congratulated by English rider Hammond, who was beaten in Roubaix velodrome. At left, the hug of Peter Van Petegem and Johan Museeuw.

Gand Wevelgem

Boonen conferms as a classics champion at
Ghent-Wevelgem

Geert Omloop

Freccia Vallone

Davide Rebellin was the hero of the Mur de Huy

39ªAmstel Gold Race

The Amstel podium. Davide Rebelllin, in center, with Miki Boogerd (left) and Paolo Bettini with his Italian Champions jersey.

Above, Rebellin on the attack with
hometown fave Miki Boogerd

Davide Rebellin

After winning the Amstel Gold Race and Freccia Vallone, Davide Rebellin finished his historic hat trick by winning Liegi-Bastogne-Liegi. Once again, he's ahead of Miki Boogerd.

Coté St.Roch

Redoute

Coté De Ans

Rebellin beats Boogerd at the finish
line in Ans

Tour de Romandie

Hamilton rules in Romandie, where Garzelli won a stage.

Giro del Trentino

Jan Svorada

Here's Cunego:
the Giro del Trentino was his first
step in a tremendous season.

Passo Carlo Magno

The Giro d'Italia passes through Puglia.
Below, Damiano Cunego kisses the
trophy of the Pink Race.
He was the winner of the '87° edition.

Bradley McGee opened the Giro by winning the prologue in Genoa. The Australian wore the first Pink Jersey in a spectacular Giro.

Nine stage wins of Alessandro Petacchi

Gilberto Simoni wins the stage to
Corno alle Scale.

Stefano Garzelli

Rinaldo Nocentini

Franco Pellizotti

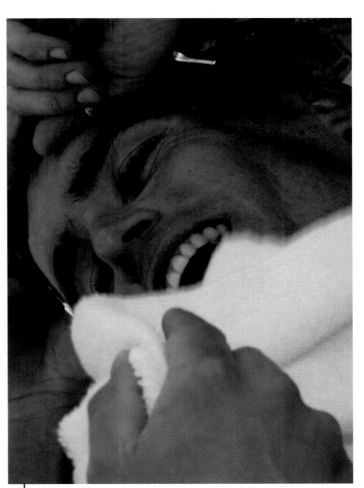

Bradley McGee

Top three timetrialists.
Above, Jaroslav Popovych, who thanks to the
Trieste time trial took over the Pink Jersey.
Right, Sergey Gonchar, who won the TT stage.
Left, Alberto Ongarato.

Snow on the Gavia. Left, Stefano Garzelli.
Above, Cunego in Pink Jersey, with Simoni,
the Green (Climbers) Jersey Wegmann.
Below, Cunego wins in Bormio 2000.

Stefano Garzelli

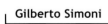

Gilberto Simoni

Dauphine Libere

Ivan Basso

Iban Mayo

Lance Armstrong

George Hincapie

Pre-Tour test at Dauphine'.
Armstrong is 4th in the French race that is
dominated by Basque Iban Mayo.

Jorg Jahsche

68°Tour de Suisse

In Switzerland, Jan Ullrich shined ahead of Fabian Jeker and Dario Cioni. Paolo Bettini, in his Italian Champion jersey, won a big stage.

Gerg Totschnig

Deutschland Tour

Jan Ullrich

Tom Boonen

Allan Davis

In the Deutschland Tour, a new talent reveals itself: Patrick Sinkewitz.

Lance Armstrong makes history.
The Texan wins his sixth consecutive Tour.
There's simply no one like him.

The prologue in Liegi was for young Fabian Cancellara. The Swiss is the first Yellow Jersey of the 2004 Tour.

Mario Cipollini

It seemed like Roubaix, but it was the fourth daay of the Tour, with a stage finish in Wasqueha . Mayo paid a major price on this stage with pave' .

Iban Mayo

Hincapie, Armstrong

Martin Hvastja

Bobby Julich

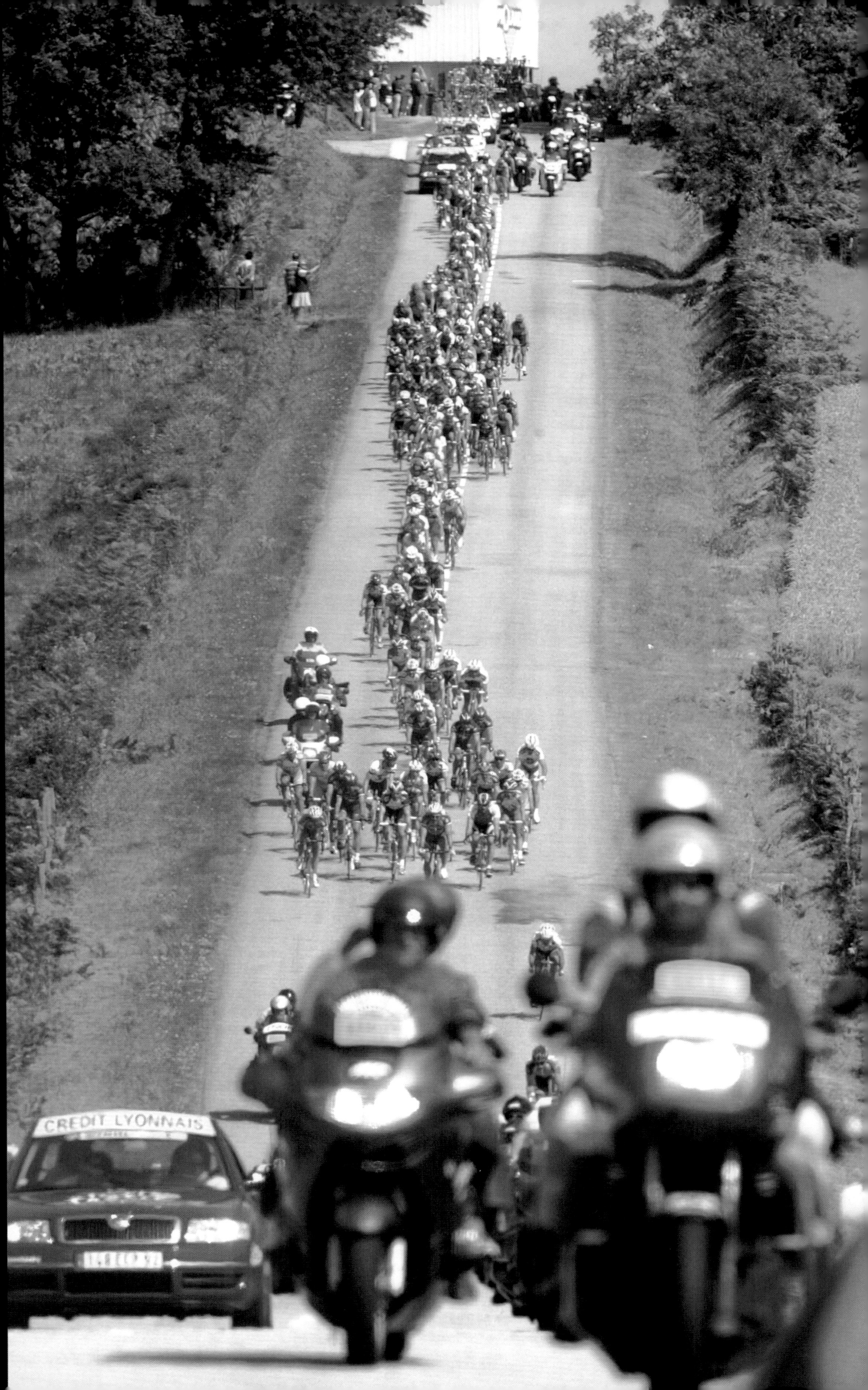
CREDIT LYONNAIS

Paolo Bettini

Mario Cipollini

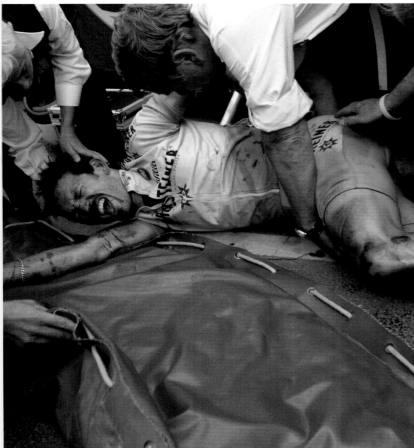

René Haselbacher

Gianmatteo Fagnini

Many falls in the first days. Above right,
Cipollini gets going after a difficult crash.
Re Leone retired after 5 stages.

The US Postal team of Armstrong dominated the team time trial in Arras and Lance had the Yellow Jersey right away. But the next day in Chartres, they left the symbol of race leadership to Thomas Voeckler (opposite page). The young Frenchman, hero of the first part of the Tour, was leader for 10 days.

Thomas Voeckler

Ivan Basso

Lance Armstrong

The podium of the 2004 Tour was decided in the mountains. Above, Lance Armstrong could count on the support of a special fan, his girlfriend Sheryl Crow. On the next page, Ivan Basso, winner at La Mongie with German champion Andreas Kloden.

Vladimir Karpets

Francisco Mancebo

Fun Time At The Tour. The Australian Robbie McEwen, with two stage wins, celebrates his Green Jersey for the Points Classification with a wheelie.

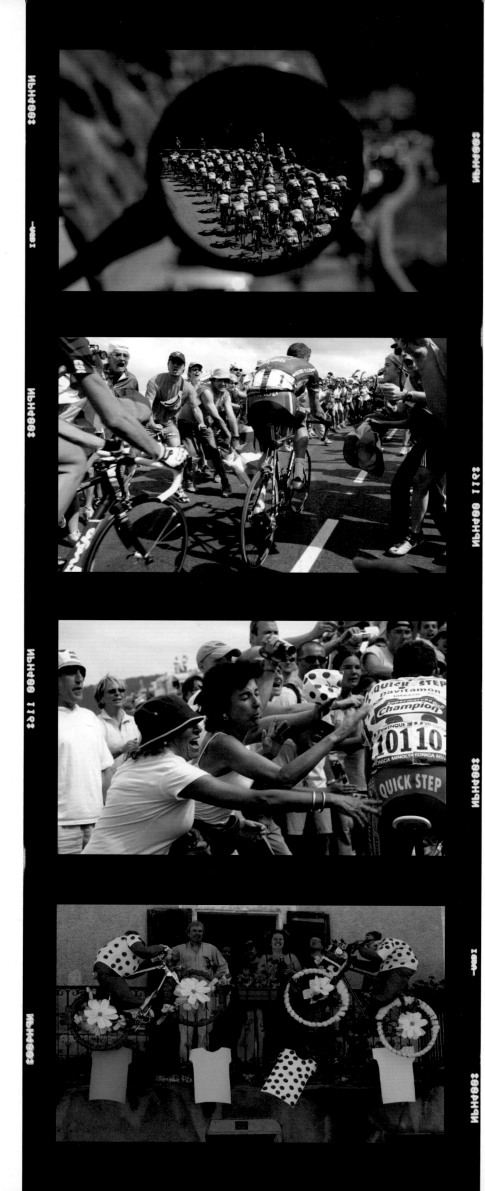

...h challeneged at the end of the Tour.
...was only 4° in the final classification.

Lance Armstrong also won the Besançon TT. The sixth Tour was his.
On the opposite page, the podium with Armstrong, Kloden and Basso.

In the duel between Bettini and Rebellin, Martin Perdiguero was able to win the Basque Classic Classicissima in a close sprint finish.

Axel Merckx

Davide Rebellin

Stuart O'Grady beats Bettini and World Champ
Astarloa in the sprint.
The Hamburg classic is Australian.

Another World Cup sprint. This time, it's the Spanish rider Juan Antonio Flecha, while Bettini is second again.

Paolo Bettini, the main favorite, wins the Olympic title in Athens.
On the podium, a surprise, the portugese Paulinho and the generous Axel Merckx.

Axel Merckx

Erik Zabel

Paolo Bettini

59ªVuelta Espana

Hat trick by Roberto Heras at the Vuelta.
In the Spanish tour, the losers were Perez
and Mancebo. Garzelli, first among
<foreign> riders was 11th.

Alessandro Valverde   Santiago Perez

Cardenas   Francisco Mancebo

Igor Astarloa

Damiano Cunego, Leonardo Piepoli

Roberto Heras

Another historic triple: Oscar Freire, already World Champion
at Verona in '99, won his third World title.
In the city of Juliette and Romeo, he beat Zabel and Paolini in the sprint.

Major festival of cycling in Verona.
Olympic champion Paolo Bettini, big favorite
had to retire due to major pain in his right knee
when he hit it against his handlebars and the
Italian team car. On the opposite page,
he's aided by Roberto Petito.

Oscar Freire

Zabel, Freire, Paolini

Under 23

Kostanstin Siutsou

Domenico Pozzovivo

Kostanstin Siutsou

Juniores

Roman Kreuziger

Rafaa Chtioui

Roman Kreuzige

Senior

Judith Arndt

Junior donne

Marianne Vos

Tatiana Guderzo

Marta Bastianelli

Francesca Andina

Guderzo, Arndt, Valen

Miss Mondiali

Janez Brajkovic

Karin Thurig

Kreuziger, Gretsch, Schadre

Tereza Hirikova

World Time Trial Championships in Bardolino.
The golds went to the Australian Mick Rogers and Swiss Karin Thurig.

98ªParis Tours

Erik Dekker, a huge win after a historic escape

98°Giro di Lombardia

Damiano Cunego confirms his super talent,
and not just in stage races. Bettini wins
the World Cup challenge with Rebellin

Basso, Cunego   Daniele Nardello

Results

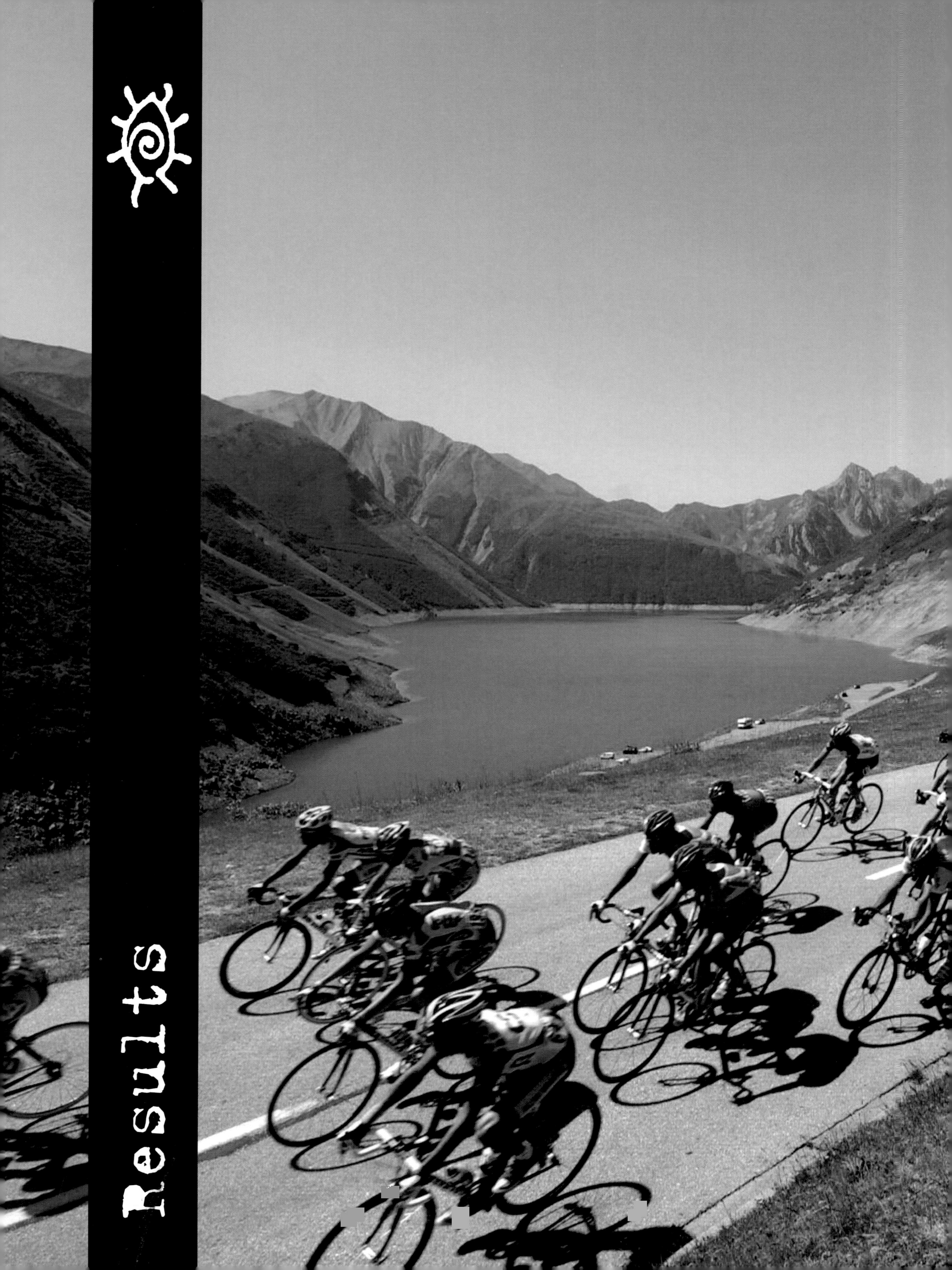

95ᵃMilano Sanremo	88ᵃRonde van Vlaanderen	102ᵃParis Roubaix	39ᵃAmstel Gold Race	90ᵃLiegie Bastogne Liegie
1 Oscar Freire Gomez (Spa-Rab) 7.11.23	**1** Steffen Wesemann (Ger-Tmo) 6.39.00	**1** Magnus Backstedt (Alb) 6.40.26	**1** Davide Rebellin (Ita-Gst) 6.23.44	**1** Davide Rebellin (Ita-Gst) 6.20.09
2 Erik Zabel (Ger-Tmo)	**2** Leif Hoste (Bel-Lot)	**2** Tristan Hoffman (Ned-Csc)	**2** Michael Boogerd (Ned-Rab)	**2** Michael Boogerd (Ned-Rab)
3 Stuart O'Grady (Aus-Cof)	**3** Dave Bruylandts (Bel-Mar)	**3** Roger Hammond (GBr-Mrb)	**3** Paolo Bettini (Ita-Qsd)	**3** Alexandre Vinokourov (Kaz-Tmo)
4 Alessandro Petacchi (Ita-Fas)	**4** Leon van Bon (Ned-Lot) 0.28	**4** Fabian Cancellara (Swi-Fas)	**4** Danilo Di Luca (Ita-Sae)	**4** Samuel Sanchez Gonzalez (Spa-Eus)
5 Max van Heeswijk (Ned-Usp)	**5** Erik Dekker (Ned-Rab)	**5** Johan Museeuw (Bel-Qsd)	**5** Peter van Petegem (Bel-Lot)	**5** Erik Dekker (Ned-Rab)
6 Igor Astarloa Askasibar (Spa-Cof)	**6** Andreas Klier (Ger-Tmo)	**6** Peter Van Petegem (Bel-Lot)	**6** Matthias Kessler (Ger-Tmo)	**6** Matthias Kessler (Ger-Tmo)
7 Romans Vainsteins (Lat-Lam)	**7** Rolf Aldag (Ger-Tmo)	**7** Leon van Bon (Ned-Lot) 0.29	**7** Erik Dekker (Ned-Rab)	**7** Michele Scarponi (Ita-Dve)
8 Paolo Bettini (Ita-Qsd)	**8** Frank Hoj (Den-Csc)	**8** George Hincapie (Usa-Usp)	**8** Serguei Ivanov (Rus-Tmo)	**8** Ivan Basso (Ita-Csc)
9 Miguel Martin Perdiguero (Spa-Sdv)	**9** Paolo Bettini (Ita-Qsd)	**9** Tom Boonen (Bel-Qsd)	**9** Mirko Celestino (Ita-Sae)	**9** Tyler Hamilton (Usa-Pho)
10 Peter Van Petegem (Bel-Lot)	**10** George Hincapie (Usa-Usp)	**10** Frank Hoy (Den-Csc)	**10** Giampaolo Caruso (Ita-Lst)	**10** Angel Vicioso Arcos (Spa-Lst)
11 Erik Dekker (Ned-Rab)	**11** Thierry Marichal (Bel-Lot)	**11** Romans Vainsteins (Lat-Lam)	**11** Oscar Camenzind (Swi-Pho)	**11** Steffen Wesemann (Ger-Tmo)
12 Mirko Celestino (Ita-Sae)	**12** Juan A.Flecha Giannoni (Spa-Fas)	**12** Leif Hoste (Bel-Lot)	**12** Luca Paolini (Ita-Qsd)	**12** David Etxebarria Alkorta (Spa-Eus)
13 George Hincapie (Usa-Usp)	**13** Laurent Brochard (Fra-A2r)	**13** Juan A.Flecha Giannoni (Spa-Fas)	**14** Axel Merckx (Bel-Lot)	**13** Eddy Mazzoleni (Ita-Sae)
14 Philippe Gilbert (Bel-FdJ)	**14** Jorg Ludewig (Ger-Sae)	**14** Ludo Dierckxsens (Bel-Lan)	**14** Oscar Freire Gomez (Spa-Rab)	**14** Oscar Freire Gomez (Spa-Rab)
15 Josu Silloniz Aresti (Spa-Eus)	**15** Jorg Ludewig (Ger-Sae)	**15** Daniele Nardello (Ita-Tmo)	**15** Michele Bartoli (Ita-Csc)	**15** Denis Menchov (Rus-Ibb)
16 Fabio Baldato (Ita-Alb)	**16** Johan Museeuw (Bel-Qsd)	**16** Steffen Wesemann (Ger-Tmo)	**16** Erik Zabel (Ger-Tmo)	**16** Frank Vandenbroucke (Bel-Fas)
17 Guido Trenti (Usa-Fas)	**17** Peter Van Petegem (Bel-Lot)	**17** Thor Hushovd (Nor-C.A)	**17** Eddy Mazzoleni (Ita-Sae)	**17** Inigo Landaluze Intxaurraga (Spa-Eus)
18 Marcus Zberg (Swi-Gst)	**18** Serguei Ivanov (Rus-Tmo)	**18** Frédéric Guesdon (Fra-FdJ)	**18** Frank Vandenbroucke (Bel-Fas)	**18** Laurent Brochard (Fra-A2r)
19 Cristian Moreni (Ita-Alb)	**19** Xavier Florencio Cabré (Spa-Reb)	**19** Serguei Ivanov (Rus-Tmo)	**19** Marcos A.Serrano Rodriguez (Spa-Lst)	**19** Floyd Landis (Usa-Usp)
20 Samuel Sanchez Gonzalez (Spa-Eus)	**20** Roberto Petito (Ita-Fas)	**20** Vladimir Gusov (Ukr-Csc)	**20** Steffen Wesemann (Ger-Tmo)	**20** Juan M.Garate Cepa (Spa-Lam)
21 Andreas Klier (Ger-Tmo)	**21** Michael Boogerd (Ned-Rab)	**21** Michele Bartoli (Ita-Csc)	**21** Nicki Sörensen (Den-Csc)	**21** Marcus Zberg (Swi-Gst)
22 Michele Gobbi (Ita-Den)	**22** Stijn Devolder (Bel-Usp)	**22** Jaan Kirsipuu (Est-A2r) 3.50	**22** Michele Scarponi (Ita-Dve)	**22** Paolo Bettini (Ita-Qsd)
23 Inigo Landaluze Intxaurraga (Spa-Eus)	**23** Jaan Kirsipuu (Est-A2r)	**23** Lars Michaelsen (Den-Csc)	**23** Martin Elmiger (Swi-Pho)	**23** Manuel Beltran Martinez (Spa-Usp)
24 Yaroslav Popovych (Ukr-Lan)	**24** Oscar Freire Gomez (Spa-Rab)	**24** Fabio Baldato (Ita-Alb)	**24** Serhiy Honchar (Ukr-Den)	**24** Mirko Celestino (Ita-Sae)
25 Allan Davis (Aus-Lst)	**25** Danilo Hondo (Ger-Gst)	**25** Christophe Mengin (Fra-FdJ)	**25** Laurent Brochard (Fra-A2r)	**25** Peter Van Petegem (Bel-Lot)

Bettini smiling about his World Cup hat-trick

9ªHew Cyclassics	24ªKlasika Ciclista San Sebastian	Züri Metzgete	98ªParis Tours	98°Giro di Lombardia
1 Stuart O'Grady (Aus-Cof) 5.51.39	1 Miguel A.Martin Perdiguero (Spa-Sdv) 5.18.35	1 Juan Ant. Flecha Giannoni (Ita-Fas) 6.13.24	1 Erik Dekker (Ned-Rab) 5.33.03	1 Damiano Cunego (Ita-Sae) 6.17.55
2 Paolo Bettini (Ita-Qsd)	2 Paolo Bettini (Ita-Qsd)	2 Paolo Bettini (Ita-Qsd)	2 Danilo Hondo (Ger-Gst)	2 Michael Boogerd (Ned-Rab)
3 Igor Astarloa Askasibar (Spa-Lam)	3 Davide Rebellin (Ita-Gst)	3 Jérôme Pineau (Fra-Blb)	3 Oscar Freire Gomez (Spa-Rab)	3 Ivan Basso (Ita-Csc)
4 Oscar Freire Gomez (Spa-Rab)	4 Marcos Serrano Rodriguez (Spa-Ibb)	4 Dmitry Fofonov (Kaz-Cof)	4 Allan Davis (Spa-Lst)	4 Cadel Evans (Aus-Tmo)
5 Gerben Löwik (Ned-Cho)	5 José Alb.Martinez Trinidad (Spa-Reb)	5 Michael Albasini (Swi-Pho)	5 Stuart O'Grady (Aus-Cof)	5 Daniele Nardello (Ita-Tmo)
6 Davide Rebellin (Ita-Gst)	6 Ivan Basso (Ita-Csc)	6 Davide Rebellin (Ita-Gst)	6 Paolo Bettini (Ita-Qsd)	6 Marzio Bruseghin (Ita-Fas)
7 Erik Zabel (Ger-Tmo)	7 Georg Totschnig (Aut-Gst)	7 Michael Barry (Can-Usp)	7 Matthias Kessler (Ger-Tmo)	7 Eddy Mazzoleni (Ita-Sae)
8 Fabrizio Guidi (Ita-Csc)	8 Rik Verbrugghe (Bel-Lot)	8 George Hincapie (Usa-Usp)	8 Uros Murn (Slo-Pho)	8 Dario Frigo (Ita-Fas)
9 Andrej Hauptman (Slo-Lam)	9 Constantino Zaballa Gutierrez (Spa-Sdv)	9 Oscar Freire Gomez (Spa-Rab)	9 Jaan Kirsipuu (Est-A2r)	9 Franco Pellizotti (Ita-Alb)
10 Paolo Bossoni (Ita-Lam)	10 Marcus Zberg (Swi-Gst)	10 Massimiliano Gentili (Ita-Dve)	10 Eddy Mazzoleni (Ita-Sae)	10 Luca Mazzanti (Ita-Pan)
11 Erik Dekker (Ned-Rab)	11 Oscar Freire Gomez (Spa-Rab)	11 Unai Yus Kerejeta (Spa-Blb)	11 Stefan Van Dijk (Ned-Lot)	11 Christopher Horner (Usa-Sdv)
12 Mirco Celestino (Ita-Sae)	12 Igor Astarloa Askasibar (Spa-Lam)	12 Rik Verbrugghe (Bel-Lot)	12 Philippe Gilbert (Bel-FdJ)	12 Erik Dekker (Ned-Rab)
13 Philippe Gilbert (Bel-FdJ)	13 Juan Ant.Flecha Giannoni (Spa-Fas)	13 Serhiy Honchar (Ukr-Den)	13 Davide Rebellin (Ita-Gst)	13 Ondrej Sosenka (Cze-A&S)
14 Matteo Tosatto (Ita-Fas)	14 Cristian Moreni (Ita-Alb)	14 Alexandr Kolobnev (Rus-Dve)	14 Alexandre Usov (Blr-Pho)	14 Isidro Nozal Vega (Spa-Lst)
15 Kim Kirchen (Lux-Fas)	15 Xavier Florencio Cabré (Spa-Reb)	15 Joseba Albizu Lizaso (Spa-Eus)	15 Cristian Moreni (Ita-Alb)	15 Giampaolo Caruso (Ita-Lst)
16 Oscar Camenzind (Swi-Pho)	16 Tadej Valjavec (Slo-Pho)	16 Marcus Zberg (Swi-Gst)	16 Peter Van Petegem (Bel-Lot)	16 Volodymir Duma (Ukr-Lan)
17 Serhiy Honchar (Ukr-Den)	17 Richard Virenque (Fra-Qsd)	17 Mirko Celestino (Ita-Sae)	17 Eric Baumann (Ger-Tmo)	17 Cédric Vasseur (Fra-Cof)
18 Laurent Brochard (Fra-A2r)	18 Mirko Celestino (Ita-Sae)	18 Ruggero Borghi (Ita-Den)	18 Anthony Geslin (Fra-Blb)	18 Serhiy Honchar (Ukr-Den)
19 Vladimir Goussev (Rus-Csc)	19 Erik Dekker (Ned-Rab)	19 David Moncoutié (Fra-Cof)	19 Inaki Isasi Flores (Spa-Eus)	19 Vladimir Goussev (Rus-Csc)
20 Axel Merckx (Bel-Lot)	20 Stefano Garzelli (Ita-Vin)	20 Serge Baguet (Bel-Lot)	20 Pablo Lastras Garcia (Spa-Ibb)	20 Joaquin Rodriguez Oliver (Spa-Sdv)
21 Matthieu Sprick (Fra-Blb)	21 Damiano Cunego (Ita-Sae)	21 Francesco Casagrande (Ita-Lam)	21 Mirko Celestino (Ita-Sae)	21 Ruslan Ivanov (Mda-Alb)
22 Michele Gobbi (Ita-Den)	22 Bobby Julich (Usa-Csc)	22 Fabian Wegmann (Ger-Gst)	22 Guido Trenti (Usa-Fas)	22 Matthias Kessler (Ger-Gst)
23 Danilo Di Luca (Ita-Sae)	23 Carlos Garcia Quesada (Spa-Kel)	23 Volodymyr Gustov (Ukr-Fas)	23 Andrej Hauptman (Slo-Lam)	23 Michael Rasmussen (Den-Rab)
24 Andrey Kashechkin (Kaz-C.A)	24 David Herrero Llorente (Spa-Alm)	24 Michele Bartoli (Ita-Csc)	24 Gert Steegmans (Bel-Lot)	24 Francisco J.Vila Errandonea (Spa-Lam)
25 Matthew White (Aus-Cof)	25 Filippo Simeoni (Ita-Dve)	25 Georg Totschnig (Aut-Gst)	25 Karsten Kroon (Ned-Rab)	25 Tomas Nose (Slo-Pho)

2004 World Cup podium: Bettini, Rebellin and Freire.
Below, T-Mobile, first in team classification.

Road World Championships

MEN: Elite - Road Race - 265,5 kms

1 Óscar Freire Gomez (Spa-Rab) 6.57.15
2 Erik Zabel (Ger-Tmo)
3 Luca Paolini (Ita-Qsd)
4 Stuart O'Grady (Aus-Cof)
5 Allan Davis (Aus-Lst)
6 Alejandro Valverde Belmonte (Spa-Kel)
7 Michael Boogerd (Ned-Rab)
8 Chris Horner (Usa-Web)
9 Damiano Cunego (Ita-Sae)
10 Frank Schleck (Lux-Csc)
11 Ivan Basso (Ita-Csc)
12 Francisco Mancebo Perez (Ibb)
13 Michael Rasmussen (Den-Rab)
14 Danilo Hondo (Ger-Gst)
15 Marcos Serrano Rodriguez (Spa-Lst
16 Alexandre Vinokourov (Kaz-Tmo) 0.05
17 Luis Perez Rodriguez (Spa-Cof) 0.09
18 Steffen Wesemann (Ger-Tmo) 0.26
19 Matthias Kessler (Ger-Tmo) 0.58
20 Karsten Kroon (Ned-Rab) 1.39
21 Mauricio Alb.Ardila Cano (Col-Cho)
22 Dario Frigo (Ita-Fas) 1.41
23 Leonardo Bertagnolli (Ita-Sae)
24 Ivan R.Parra Pinto (Col-Baq) 3.09
25 Dmitri Konychev (Rus-Lpr) 4.26
26 Martin Elmiger (Swi-Pho)
27 Erki Pütsep (Est-A2r)
28 Mikhaylo Khalilov (Ukr-Ict)
29 Peter Van Petegem (Bel-Lot)
30 Uros Murn (Slo-Pho)
31 Geert Verheyen (Bel-Cho)
32 Jérôme Pineau (Fra-Blb)
33 Fabian Wegmann (Ger-Gst)
34 Cezary Zamana (Pol-Cho)
35 Grégory Rast (Swi-Pho)
36 Luis F.Laverde Jimenez (Col-Fpf)
37 Kurt-Asle Arvesen (Nor-Csc)
38 Roger Beuchat (Swi-Vin)
39 Nicki Sörensen (Den-Csc)
40 Alexandre Botcharov (Rus-C.A)
41 Harald Morscher (Aut-Vol)
42 Matej Mugerli (Slo-Vin-stag)
43 Daniel Schnider (Swi-Pho)
44 Ruslan Ivanov (Mda-Alb)
45 Constantino Zaballa Gutierrez (Spa-Sdv)
46 David Moncoutié (Fra-Cof)
47 Freddy E.Gonzalez Martinez (Col-Clm)
48 Nicolas Vogondy (Fra-FdJ)
49 Igor Pugaci (Mda-Den)
50 David O'Loughlin (Irl-*El.2)

MEN: Under 23 - Road Race = 177 kms

1 Kanstantsin Siutsou (Blr) 4.33.33
2 Thomas Dekker (Ned) 1.01
3 Mads Christensen (Den) 1.02
4 Domenico Pozzovivo (Ita) 1.09
5 Vincenzo Nibali (Ita) 1.30
6 Matti Breschel (Den) 1.38
7 Giovanni Visconti (Ita)
8 Marc de Maar (Ned) 1.41
9 Andreas Dietziker (Swi) 1.50
10 Nick Ingels (Bel) 1.51

MEN: Junior - Road Race = 133 kms

1 Roman Kreuziger (Cze) 3.25.39
2 Rafaâ Chtioui (Tun)
3 Simon Spilak (Slo) 0.06
4 Eros Capecchi (Ita)
5 Pieter Jacobs (Bel)
6 Robert Gesink (Ned)
7 Ben Hermans (Bel)
8 Alexandre Binet (Fra) 0.32
9 Ivan Rovnyi (Rus)
10 Cyril Gautier (Fra)

WOMEN: Junior - Road Race = 74 kms

1 Marianne Vos (Ned) 2.11.44
2 Marta Bastianelli (Ita) 0.30
3 Eleanora van Dijk (Ned)
4 Olena Andruk (Ukr)
5 Roxane Knetemann (Ned)
6 Daiva Tuslaite (Ltu)
7 Ekaterina Tretiakova (Rus)
8 Savrina Bernardi (Ita)
9 Amanda Spratt (Aus)
10 Suzanne van Veen (Ned)

WOMEN: Elite - Road Race = 133 kms

1 Judith Arndt (Ger) 3.44.38
2 Tatiana Guderzo (Ita) 0.10
3 Anita Valen (Nor) 0.12
4 Trixi Worrack (Ger)
5 Modesta Vzesniauskaite (Ltu)
6 Nicole Brändli (Swi)
7 Joane Somarriba Arrola (Spa)
8 Svetlana Bubnenkova (Rus)
9 Mirjam Melchers (Ned)
10 Edita Pucinskaite (Ltu)

MEN: Elite - Time Trial = 46,750 kms

1 Michael Rogers (Aus-Qsd) 57.30.12
2 Michael Rich (Ger-Gst) 1.12
3 Alexandre Vinokourov (Kaz-Tmo) 1.25
4 Gustav Eric Larsson (Swe-Fas) 1.34
5 David Zabriski (Usa-Usp) 1.36
6 Marzio Bruseghin (Ita-Fas) 1.37
7 Marc Wauters (Bel-Rab) 1.56
8 Fabian Cancellara (Swi-Fas) 2.10
9 José I.Gutiérrez Palacios (Spa-Ibb) 2.23
10 Uwe Peschel (Ger-Gst) 2.28

MEN: Under 23 - Time Trial = 36,750 kms

1 Janez Brajkovic (Slo) 46.56
2 Thomas Dekker (Ned) 0.18.93
3 Vincenzo Nibali (Ita) 0.19.32
4 Dominique Cornu (Bel) 0.21
5 Christian Müller (Ger) 0.48
6 Francesco Rivera (Ita) 1.01
7 Piotr Mazur (Pol) 1.22
8 Andriy Grivko (Ukr) 1.23
9 Lukasz Bodnar (Pol) 1.27
10 Stanislav Belov (Rus) 1.33

MEN: Junior - Time Trial = 24,050 kms

1 Patrick Gretsch (Ger) 30.29
2 Roman Kreuziger (Cze) 0.15
3 Stefan Schäfer (Ger) 0.16
4 Michael Schär (Swi) 0.17
5 Viktor Renäng (Swe) 0.18
6 Alexandr Pliuschin (Mda) 0.29
7 Anders Berendt Hansen (Den) 0.37
8 Robert Gesink (Ned) 0.37
9 Alexander Slivkin (Rus) 0.43
10 Jerome Coppel (Fra) 0.49

WOMEN: Elite - Time Trial = 24,050 kms

1 Karin Thürig (Swi) 30.53
2 Judith Arndt (Ger) 0.52
3 Zoulfia Zabirova (Rus) 0.57
4 Joane Somarriba Arrola (Spa) 1.16
5 Edita Pucinskaite (Ltu) 1.32
6 Mirjam Melchers (Ned) 1.37
7 Christine Thorburn (Usa) 1.44
8 Priska Doppmann (Swi) 1.55
9 Oenone Wood (Aus 2.08
10 Tatiana Guderzo (Ita) 2.12

WOMEN: Junior - Time Trial = 15,3 kms

1 Tereza Hurikova (Cze) 22.14
2 Rebecca Much (Usa) 0.05
3 Amanda Spratt (Aus) 0.05
4 Sabine Fischer (Ger) 0.51
5 Marianne Vos (Ned) 0.55
6 Roxane Knetemann (Ned) 0.58
7 Alexandra Sontheimer (Ger) 1.01
8 Natasha Mapley (Aus) 1.09
9 Irina Zemlyanskaya (Rus) 1.13
10 Emmanuelle Merlot (Fra) 1.19

87°Giro d'Italia   91°Tour de France   59ªVuelta Espana

TAPPE

prol. prologo - Genova = Ind. Time Trial, Bradley McGee (Aus-FdJ)
1 Genova – Alba, Alessandro Petacchi (Ita-Fas)
2 Novi Ligure - Pontremoli, Lunigiana, Damiano Cunego (Ita-Sae)
3 Pontremoli - Corno Alle Scale, Gilberto Simoni (Ita-Sae)
4 Porretta Terme - Civitella in Val Di Chiana, Alessandro Petacchi (Ita-Fas)
5 Civitella in Val Di Chiana – Spoleto, Robbie McEwen (Aus-Lot)
6 Spoleto – Valmontone, Alessandro Petacchi (Ita-Fas)
7 Frosinone - Montevergine Di Mercogliano, Damiano Cunego (Ita-Sae)
8 Giffoni Valle Piana – Policoro, Alessandro Petacchi (Ita-Fas)
9 Policoro – Carovigno, Fred Rodriguez (Usa-A&S)
10 Porto Sant'Elpidio - Ascoli Piceno, Alessandro Petacchi (Ita-Fas)
11 Porto Sant'Elpidio – Cesena, Emanuele Sella (Ita-Pan)
12 Cesena – Treviso, Alessandro Petacchi (Ita-Fas)
13 Trieste - Altopiano Carsico = Ind. Time Trial, Serhiy Honchar (Ukr-Den)
14 Trieste - Pula/Pola, Alessandro Petacchi (Ita-Fas)
15 Porec/Parenzo - San Vendemiano, Alessandro Petacchi (Ita-Fas)
16 San Vendemiano – Falzes, Damiano Cunego (Ita-Sae)
rest day
17 Brunico - Fondo Sarnonico, Pavel Tonkov (Rus-Vin)
18 Cles Val di Non - Bormio 2000, Damiano Cunego (Ita-Sae)
19 Bormio – Presolana, Stefano Garzelli (Ita-Vin)
20 Clusone – Milano, Alessandro Petacchi (Ita-Fas)

TAPPE

prologue - Liège = Ind. Time Trial, Fabian Cancellara (Swi-Fas)
1 - Liège – Charleroi, Jaan Kirsipuu (Est-A2r)
2 - Charleroi – Namur, Robbie McEwen (Aus-Lot)
3 - Waterloo (Bel) - Wasquehal (Fra), Jean-Patrick Nazon (Fra-A2r)
4 - Cambrai - Arras = Team Time Trial, US Postal-Berry Floor
5 - Amiens – Chartres, Stuart O'Grady (Aus-Cof)
6 - Bonneval – Angers, Tom Boonen (Bel-Qsd)
7 - Châteaubriant - Saint-Brieuc, Filippo Pozzato (Ita-Fas)
8 - Lamballe – Quimper, Thor Hushovd (Nor-C.A)
9 - Saint-Léonard-de-Noblat – Guéret, Robbie McEwen (Aus-Lot)
10 - Limoges - Saint-Flour, Richard Virenque (Fra-Qsd)
11 - Saint-Flour – Figeac, David Moncoutié (Fra-Cof)
12 - Castelsarrasin - La Mongie , Ivan Basso (Ita-Csc)
13 - Lannemezan - Plateau de Beille, Lance Armstrong (Usa-Usp)
14 - Carcassonne – Nîmes, Aitor Gonzalez Jimenez (Ita-Fas)
15 - Valréas - Villard-de-Lans, Lance Armstrong (Usa-Usp)
16 - Bourg-d'Oisans - L'Alpe-d'Huez, Lance Armstrong (Usa-Usp)
17 - Bourg-d'Oisans - Le Grand Bornand, Lance Armstrong (Usa-Usp)
18 - Annemasse - Lons-le-Saunier , Juan M.Mercado Martin (Spa-Qsd)
19 - Besançon - Besançon = Ind. Time Trial, Lance Armstrong (Usa-Usp)
20 - Montereau – Paris, Tom Boonen (Bel-Qsd)

TAPPE

1 León - León = Team Time Trial, US Postal-Berry Floor
2 León – Burgos, Alessandro Petacchi (Ita-Fas)
3 Burgos - Soria , Alejandro Valverde Belmonte (Spa-Kel)
4 Soria – Zaragoza,. Alessandro Petacchi (Ita-Fas)
5 Zaragoza – Morella, Denis Menchov (Rus-Ibb)
6 Benicarló - Castellón de la Plana, Oscar Freire Gomez (Spa-Rab)
7 Castellón de la Plana – Valencia, Alessandro Petacchi (Ita-Fas)
8 Almussafes - Almussafes = Ind. Time Trial, Tyler Hamilton (Usa-Pho)
9 Xátiva - Alto de Aitana , Leonardo Piepoli (Ita-Sdv)
10 Alcoi - Xorret de Catí , Eladio Jimenez Sanchez (Spa-Kel)
11 San Vicente del Raspeig - Caravaca de la Cruz., David Zabriskie (Usa-Usp)
12 Almería - Calar Alto, Roberto Heras Hernandez (Spa-Lst)
13 El Ejido - Málaga , Alessandro Petacchi (Ita-Fas)
14 Málaga – Granada, Santiago Perez Fernandez (Spa-Pho)
15 Grananda - Sierra Nevada (Pradollano), Santiago Perez Fernandez (Spa-Pho)
16 Olivenza – Cáceres, José Cayetano Julia Cegarra (Spa-Kel)
17 Plasencia - Estación de Esqui La Covatilla, Felix Cardenas Ravalo (Col-Baq)
18 Béjar – Avila, Javier Pascual Rodriguez (Spa-Kel)
19 Avila - Collado Villalba, Constantino Zaballa Gutier.(Spa-Sdv)
20 Alcobendas - Puerto de Navacerrada / Valdesqui , José Enr. Gutierrez Cataluna (Spa-Pho)

FINAL CLASSIFICATION

1 Damiano Cunego (Ita-Sae) 88.40.43
2 Serhiy Honchar (Ukr-Den) 2.02
3 Gilberto Simoni (Ita-Sae) 2.05
4 Dario David Cioni (Ita-Fas) 4.36
5 Yaroslav Popovych (Ukr-Lan) 5.05
6 Stefano Garzelli (Ita-Vin) 5.31
7 Wladimir Belli (Ita-Lam) 6.12
8 Bradley McGee (Aus-FdJ) 6.15
9 Tadej Valjavec (Slo-Pho) 6.34
10 Juan M.Garate Cepa (Spa-Lam) 7.47
11 Franco Pellizotti (Ita-Alb) 9.45
12 Emanuele Sella (Ita-Pan) 10.26
13 Pavel Tonkov (Rus-Vin) 10.43
14 Christophe Brandt (Bel-Lot) 10.50
15 Luis F.Laverde Jimenez (Col-Fpf) 13.43
16 Ruben Lobato Elvira (Spa-Sdv) 21.11
17 Andrea Noè (Ita-Alb) 22.33
18 David Canada Gracia (Spa-Sdv) 22.52
19 Steve Zampieri (Swi-Vin) 25.53
20 Giuseppe Di Grande (Ita-Fpf) 26.05
21 Eddy Mazzoleni (Ita-Sae) 27.44
22 Francisco Vila Errandonea (Spa-Lam) 30.50
23 Ruggero Marzoli (Ita-A&S) 31.41
24 Vladimir Miholjevic (Cro-Alb) 32.06
25 Cristian Moreni (Ita-Alb) 35.24

FINAL CLASSIFICATION

1 Lance Armstrong (Usa-Usp) 83.36.02
2 Andreas Klöden (Ger-Tmo) 06.19
3 Ivan Basso (Ita-Csc) 06.40
4 Jan Ullrich (Ger-Tmo) 08.50
5 José Azevedo (Por-Usp) 14.30
6 Francisco Mancebo Pérez (Spa-Ibb) 18.01
7 Georg Totschnig (Aut-Gst) 18.27
8 Carlos Sastre Candil (Spa-Csc) 19.51
9 Levi Leipheimer (Usa-Rab) 20.12
10 Oscar Pereiro Sio (Spa-Pho) 22.54
11 Pietro Caucchioli (Ita-Alb) 24.21
12 Christophe Moreau (Fra-C.A) 24.36
13 Vladimir Karpets (Rus-Ibb) 25.11
14 Michael Rasmussen (Den-Rab) 27.16
15 Richard Virenque (Fra-Qsd) 28.11
16 Sandy Casar (Fra-FdJ) 28.53
17 Gilberto Simoni (Ita-Sae) 29.00
18 Thomas Voeckler (Fra-Blb) 31.12
19 Jose L.Rubiera Vigil (Spa-Usp) 32.50
20 Stéphane Goubert (Fra-A2r) 37.11
21 Axel Merckx (Bel-Lot) 39.54
22 Michael Rogers (Aus-Qsd) 41.39
23 Floyd Landis (Usa-Usp) 42.55
24 Oscar Sevilla Ribera (Spa-Pho) 45.19
25 Giuseppe Guerini (Ita-Tmo) 47.07

FINAL CLASSIFICATION

1 Roberto Heras Hernandez (Spa-Lst) 77.42.46
2 Santiago Perez Fernandez (Spa-Pho) 30
3 Francisco Mancebo Perez (Spa-Ibb) 2.13
4 Alejandro Valverde Belmonte (Spa-Kel) 3.30
5 Carlos Garcia Quesada (Spa-Kel) 7.44
6 Carlos Sastre Candil (Spa-Csc) 8.11
7 Isidro Nozal Vega (Spa-Lst) 8.32
8 José A.Gomez Marchante (Spa-Alm) 13.08
9 Luis Perez Rodriguez (Spa-Cof) 13.24
10 David Blanco Rodriguez (Spa-Kel) 15.15
11 Stefano Garzelli (Ita-Vin) 16.33
12 Marcos Serrano Rodriguez (Spa-Lst) 17.14
13 Manuel Beltran Martinez (Spa-Usp) 17.43
14 Francisco J.Lara Ruiz (Spa-Alm) 24.16
15 Samuel Sanchez Gonzalez (Spa-Eus) 29.23
16 Damiano Cunego (Ita-Sae) 29.51
17 Jorge Ferrio Luque (Spa-Alm) 30.49
18 David Plaza Romero (Spa-Baq) 31.24
19 Eladio Jimenez Sanchez (Spa-Kel) 34.35
20 Luis Pasamontes Rodriguez (Spa-Reb) 37.49
21 Unai Oza Eizaguirre (Spa-Ibb) 38.06
22 Oscar Sevilla Ribera (Spa-Pho) 39.01
23 Juan M.Garate Cepa (Spa-Lam) 40.09
24 Joan Horrach Rippoll (Spa-Ibb) 46.17
25 Daniel Atienza Urendez (Spa-Cof) 48.29

7-14.03: PARIS-NICE 2004
1 Chaville - Vanves
Jörg Jaksche (Ger-Csc)
2 Chaville - Montargis
Pedro Horillo Munoz (Spa-Qsd)
3 La Chapelle St Ursin - Roanne
Leon van Bon (Ned-Lot)
4 Roanne - Le Puy en Velay
cancelled due to bad weather
5 Le Puy en Velay - Rasteau
Alexandre Vinokourov (Kaz-Mob)
6 Rasteau - Gap
Denis Menchov (Rus-Ibb)
7 Digne les Bains - Cannes
Alexandre Vinokourov (Kaz-Mob)
8 Nice - Nice
Alexandre Vinokourov (Kaz-Mob)

FINAL CLASSIFICATION

1 Jörg Jaksche (Ger-Csc)
2 David Rebellin (Ita-Gst)
3 Bobby Julich (Usa-Csc)
4 Jens Voigt (Ger-Csc)
5 George Hincapie (Usa-Usp)
6 Frank Vandenbroucke (Bel-Fas)
7 Oscar Pereiro Sio (Spa-Pho)
8 Michael Rogers (Aus-Qsd)
9 Frank Schleck (Lux-Csc)
10 José Azevedo (Por-Usp)

10-16.03: TIRRENO ADRIATICO 2004
1 Sabaudia - Sabaudia
Alessandro Petacchi (Ita-Fas)
2 Latina - Maddaloni
Alessandro Petacchi (Ita-Fas)
3 Maddaloni - Isernia
Oscar Freire Gomez (Spa-Rab)
4 Isernia - Paglieta
Paolo Bettini (Ita-Qsd)
5 Paglieta - Torricella Sicura
Roberto Petito (Ita-Fas)
6 Monte San Pietrangeli-Torre S.Patrizio
Paolo Bettini (Ita-Qsd)
7 S.Benedetto Del Tronto -
S.Benedetto Del Tronto
Alessandro Petacchi (Ita-Fas)

FINAL CLASSIFICATION

1 Paolo Bettini (Ita-Qsd)
2 Oscar Freire Gomez (Spa-Rab)
3 Erik Zabel (Ger-Mob)
4 Igor Astarloa Askasibar (Spa-Cof)
5 Stuart O'Grady (Aus-Cof)
6 Michael Boogerd (Ned-Rab)
7 Rolf Aldag (Ger-Mob)
8 Giuliano Figueras (Ita-Pan)
9 Angel Vicioso Arcos (Spa-Lst)
10 Joaquin Rodriguez Oliver (Spa-Sdv)

5-9.04: Vuelta a Pais Vasco
1 Bergara - Bergara
Alejandro Valverde Belmonte (Spa-Kel)
2 Bargara - Zalla
Beat Zberg (Swi-Gst)
3 Zalla - Vitoria
Carlos Zarate Fernandez (Spa-Kel)
4 Gazteiz - Lekunberri
Denis Menchov (Rus-Ibb)
5A Lekunberri - Lazkao
Jens Voigt (Ger-Csc)
5B Lazkao = Ind. Time Trial
Bobby Julich (Usa-Csc)

FINAL CLASSIFICATION

1 Denis Menchov (Rus-Ibb)
2 Iban Mayo Diez (Spa-Eus)
3 David Etxebarria Alkorta (Spa-Eus)
4 Bobby Julich (Usa-Csc)
5 Levi Leipheimer (Usa-Rab)
6 Alejandro Valverde Belmonte (Spa-Kel)
7 Floyd Landis (Usa-Usp)
8 Samuel Sanchez Gonzalez (Spa-Eus)
9 Koldo Gil Perez (Spa-Lst)
10 Jorge Ferrio Luque (Spa-Alm)

**07.04: Gent - Wevelgem - Bel - Hors.
- 204 km**

1 Tom Boonen (Bel-Qsd)
2 Magnus Backstedt (Swe-Alb)
3 Jaan Kirsipuu (Est-A2r)
4 George Hincapie (Usa-Usp)
5 Jimmy Casper (Fra-Cof)
6 Roger Hammond (GBr-Mrb)
7 Juan A.Flecha Giannoni (Spa-Fas)
8 Vladimir Goussev (Rus-Csc)

9 Sébastien Rosseler (Bel-Reb)
10 Andreas Klier (Ger-Tmo)

**21.04: La Flèche Wallonne - Bel
– 199,5 km**

1 Davide Rebellin (Ita-Gst)
2 Danilo Di Luca (Ita-Sae)
3 Matthias Kessler (Ger-Tmo)
4 Michele Scarponi (Ita-Dve)
5 Alexandre Vinokourov (Kaz-Tmo)
6 Andreas Klöden (Ger-Tmo)
7 Frank Vandenbroucke (Bel-Fas)
8 Marcos Serrano Rodriguez (Spa-Lst)
9 Marcus Zberg (Swi-Gst)
10 Manuel Beltran Martinez (Spa-Usp)

27.04-02.05: Tour de Romandie
Prologue: Geneva
Bradley McGee (Aus-FdJ)
1 Yverdon-les-Bains - Yverdon-les-Bains
Jan Svorada (Cze-Lam)
2 Romont - Romont
Stefano Garzelli (Ita-Vin)
3 Romont - Morgins
Alexandre Moos (Swi-Pho)
4 Sion - Sion
Fabian Jeker (Swi-Sdv)
5 Lausanne - Lausanne = Ind. Time Trial
Tyler Hamilton (Usa-Pho)

FINAL CLASSIFICATION

1 Tyler Hamilton (Usa-Pho)
2 Fabian Jeker (Swi-Sdv)
3 Leonardo Piepoli (Ita-Sdv)
4 Tadej Valjavec (Slo-Pho)
5 David Dario Cioni (Ita-Fas)
6 Alexandre Moos (Swi-Pho)
7 Ivan Basso (Ita-Csc)
8 Francisco Mancebo Perez (Spa-Ibb)
9 Bradley McGee (Aus-FdJ)
10 Steve Zampieri (Swi-Vin)

6-17.06: Dauphiné Libéré
Prologue: Megève - Megève
Iban Mayo Diez (Spa-Eus)
1 Megève - Bron
Thor Hushovd (Nor-C.A)
2 Bron - Saint-Étienne
José Enr.Gutierrez Cataluna (Spa-Pho)
3 Saint-Étienne - Aubenas
Nicolas Portal (Fra-A2r)
4 Bédoin - Mont Ventoux
Iban Mayo Diez (Spa-Eus)
5 Bollène - Sisteron
Stuart O'Grady (Aus-Cof)
6 Gap - Grenoble
Michael Rasmussen (Den-Rab)
7 Grenoble - Grenoble
Stuart O'Grady (Aus-Cof)

FINAL CLASSIFICATION

1 Iban Mayo Diez (Spa-Eus)
2 Tyler Hamilton (Usa-Pho)
3 Oscar Sevilla Ribera (Spa-Pho)
4 Lance Armstrong (Usa-Usp)
5 Juan M.Mercado Martin (Spa-Qsd)
6 José Enr.Gutierrez Cataluna (Spa-Pho)

7 Michael Rasmussen (Den-Rab)
8 Levi Leipheimer (Usa-Rab)
9 Oscar Pereiro Sio (Spa-Pho)
10 Inigo Landaluze Intxaurraga(Spa-Eus)

14-20.06: Vuelta a Catalunya
1 Salou - Salou = Team Time Trial
TTT = Illes Balears-Banesto
2 Salou - Horta de Saint Joan
Miguel A.Martin Perdiguero (Spa-Sdv)

3 Les Borges Blanques - Andorra (Coll de Pal)
Miguel A.Martin Perdiguero (Spa-Sdv)
4 Llorts (Andorra) - Ordino-Arcalis
Miguel A.Martin Perdiguero (Spa-Sdv)
5 Liivia - Blanes
Danilo Hondo (Ger-Gst)
6 Blanes - Vallirana
Max van Heeswijk (Ned-Usp)
7 Olesa de Montserrat - Barcelona
Isaac Galvez Lopez (Spa-Ibb)

FINAL CLASSIFICATION

1 Miguel A.Martin Perdiguero (Spa-Sdv)
2 Vladimir Karpets (Rus-Ibb)
3 Roberto Laiseka Jaio (Spa-Eus)
4 David Latasa Lasa (Spa-Kel)
5 Eladio Jimenez Sanchez (Spa-Kel)
6 Ivan R.Parra Pinto (Col-Kel)
7 Alberto Lopez de Munain (Spa-Eus)
8 Josep Jufré Pou (Spa-Reb)
9 Pablo Lastras Garcia (Spa-Ibb)
10 Daniel Atienza Urendez (Spa-Cof)

12-20.06: Tour de Suisse 2004
1 Sursee - Beromünster
Jan Ullrich (Ger-Tmo)
2 Dürrenroth - Rheinfelden
Robbie McEwen (Aus-Lot)
3 Rheinfelden - Juraparc-Vallorbe
Robert Hunter (Rsa-Rab)
4 Vallée de Joux - Bätterkinden
Robbie McEwen (Aus-Lot)
5 Bätterkinden - Adelboden
Robert Hunter (Rsa-Rab)
6 Frutigen - Linthal
Niki Aebersold (Swi-Pho)
7 Linthal - Malbun (Lie)
Georg Totschnig (Aut-Gst)
8 Buchs - Bellinzone
Paolo Bettini (Ita-Qsd)
9 Lugano - Lugano = Ind.Time Trial
Jan Ullrich (Ger-Tel)

FINAL CLASSIFICATION

1 Jan Ullrich (Ger-Tmo)
2 Fabian Jeker (Swi-Sdv)
3 Dario David Cioni (Ita-Fas)
4 Georg Totschnig (Aut-Gst)
5 Evgueni Petrov (Rus-Sae)
6 Txema.Del Olmo Zendegi (Spa-Mil)
7 Patrik Sinkewitz (Ger-Qsd)
8 Giuseppe Guerini (Ita-Tmo)
9 Oscar Camenzind (Swi-Pho)
10 David Canada Gracia (Spa-Sdv)

29.08: GP Ouest-France Plouay - Fra

1 Didier Rous (Fra-Blb)
2 Serge Baguet (Bel-Lot)
3 Guido Trentin (Ita-Cof)
4 Danilo Hondo (Ger-Gst)
5 Giulio Tomi (Ita-Vin)
6 Vladimir Duma (Ukr-Lan)
7 Patrick Calcagni (Swi-Vin)
8 Cédric Vasseur (Fra-Cof)
9 Sergio Barbero (Ita-Lam)
10 Fabian Wegmann (Ger-Gst)

18.09: Giro del Lazio - Ita

1 Juan Ant.Flecha Giannoni (Ita-Fas)
2 Gilberto Simoni (Ita-Sae)
3 Jan Ullrich (Ger-Tmo)
4 Marco Serpellini (Ita-Gst)
5 Rinaldo Nocentini (Ita-A&S)
6 Massimo Giunti (Ita-Dve)
7 Gabriele Missaglia (Ita-Tbl)
8 Dario Frigo (Ita-Fas)
9 Andrea Noè (Ita-Alb)
10 Luca Mazzanti (Ita-Pan)

20-25.01: Tour Down Under-Aus- 2.3
1 East End Adelaide Street Race
Robbie McEwen (Aus-Lot)
2 Norwood - Kapunda
David McPartland (Aus-Ten)
3 Goolwa - Victor Harbor
Philippe Gilbert (Bel-FdJ)
4 Unley - Hahndorf
Robbie McEwen (Aus-Lot)
5 Willunga - Willunga
Benjamin Day (Aus-Pal)
6 Adelaide City Council Circuit
Baden Cooke (Aus-FdJ)

FINAL CLASSIFICATION
1 Patrick Jonker (Aus-*El.2)
2 Robbie McEwen (Aus-Lot)
3 Baden Cooke (Aus-FdJ)

31.01: Doha International GP-Qat- 1.3
Simone Cadamuro (Ita-Den)

01.02: Trofeo Mallorca-Spa- 1.3
Allan Davis (Aus-Lst)

02.02: Trofeo Alcudia-Spa- 1.3
Oscar Freire Gomez (Spa-Rab)

02-06.02: Tour de Qatar-Qat- 2.3
1 Sealine Beach Resort-Doha Landmark
Francisco Ventoso Alberdi (Spa-Sdv)
2 Al Zubarah-Doha Hyatt Plaza
Tom Boonen (Bel-Qsd)
3 Camel Race Track
Robert Hunter (Rsa-Rab)
4 Al Wakra - Al Wakra
Fabian Cancellara (Swi-Fas)
5 Doha Golf Club-Doha Corniche
Robert Hunter (Rsa-Rab)

FINAL CLASSIFICATION
1 Robert Hunter (Rsa-Rab)
2 Robbie McEwen (Aus-Lot)
3 Tom Boonen (Bel-Qsd)

03.02: Trofeo Cala Millor-Spa-150 kms 1.3
Alejandro Valverde Belmonte (Spa-Kel)

03.02: GP Ouv. La Marseillaise-Fra-150 km 1.3
Baden Cooke (Aus-FdJ)

04.02: Trofeo Manacor-Spa-159,8 kms 1.3
Allan Davis (Aus-Lst)

04-08.02: Etoile de Bessèges-Fra 2.3
1 Marseille-Marseille
Tom Steels (Bel-Lan)
2 GP Palavas les Flots
Jaan Kirsipuu (Est-A2r)
3 Nîmes-Casino les Fumades
Thor Hushovd (Nor-C.A)
4 Branoux les Taillades-Salles du Gardon
Laurent Brochard (Fra-A2r)
5 GP Bessèges
Jaan Kirsipuu (Est-A2r)

FINAL CLASSIFICATION
1 Laurent Brochard (Fra-A2r)
2 Sylvain Calzati (Fra-Okt)
3 Joseba Zubeldia Aguirre (Spa-Eus)

05.02: Trofeo Calvia-Spa-148,3 kms 1.3
Unai Etxebarria Arana (Ven-Eus)

06-15.02: Tour de Langkawi-Mas- 2.2
1 Penang - Taiping
Merculio Ramos - (PHI19780423)
2 Ipoh - Tanah Rata
Marlon Perez Arango (Col-Clm)
3 Tapah - Raub
Brett Lancaster (Aus-Pan)
4 Ulu Kelang - Tampin
Sean Sullivan (Aus-Tbl)
5 Melaka
Eric Wohlberg (Can-Sie)
6 Muar - Johor Bahru
Ivan Quaranta (Ita-Fpf)
7 Pontian - Melaka
Luciano Pagliarini Mendonca (Bra-Lam)
8 Port Dickson - Shah Alam
Luciano Pagliarini Mendonca (Bra-Lam)
9 Menara Telekom, KL - Genting Highlands
Ruber Marin Valencia (Col-Clm)
10 Kuala Lumpur Criterium
Ruben Guillermo Bongiorno (Arg-Pan)

FINAL CLASSIFICATION
1 Freddy Gonzalez Martinez (Col-Clm)
2 Ryan Cox (Rsa-Tbl)
3 Dave Bruylandts (Bel-Cho)

08.02 Costa degli Etruschi-Ita- 197,3 kms 1.3
Yuri Mitlushenko (Ukr-Lan)

Igor Astarloa

13-15.02: Giro della Liguria-Ita-134 km 1.3
Filippo Pozzato (Ita-Fas)

15-19.02: Vuelta a Andalucia-Spa- 2.3
1 Huelva - Sevilla
Tom Boonen (Bel-Qsd)
2 Arcos de la Frontera-Benalmadena Costa
Max Van Heeswijk (Ned-Usp)
3 Humilladero-Alto Virgen de la Sierra (Cabra)
Juan Carlos Domingues (Spa-Sdv)
4 Lucena - Jaen
Max Van Heeswijk (Ned-Usp)
5 La Zubia - Almeria
Erik Zabel (Ger-Mob)

FINAL CLASSIFICATION
1 Juan Carlos Domínguez (Spa-Sdv)
2 Carlos García Quesada (Spa-Kel)
3 Samuel Sánchez González (Spa-Eus)

17.02: Trofeo Laigueglia-Ita-183,3 km 1.2
Filippo Pozzato (Ita-Fas)

Max Van Heeswijk

08-10.02: GP CTT Correios de Portugal -Por- 2.3
1 Santiago do Cacém-Santiago do Cacém
Candido Barbosa (Por-Lap)
2 Sines - Beja
José A.Gomez Marchante (Spa-Alm)
3 Beja - Loulé
Candido Barbosa (Por-Lap)

FINAL CLASSIFICATION
1 Candido Barbosa (Por-Lap)
2 Angel Edo Alsina (Spa-Mil)
3 Alberto Benito Guerreiro (Spa-Ant)

11-15.02: Tour Méditerranéen-Fra 2.3
1 Le Cannet - Mentone
Baden Cooke (Aus-FdJ)
2 La Londe des Maures – Hyères
Paolo Bettini (Ita-Qsd)
3 Rousset - Berre l'Etang
Baden Cooke (Aus-FdJ)
4 Greasque - Marignane
Mario Cipollini (Ita-Dve)
5 La Garde -Toulon Mont Faron
Jörg Jaksche (Ger-Csc)

FINAL CLASSIFICATION
1 Jörg Jaksche (Ger-Csc)
2 Ivan Basso (Ita-Csc)
3 Jens Voigt (Ger-Csc)

18-22.02: Volta ao Algarve-Por- 2.3
1 Albufeira - Albufeira
Alberto Benito Guerreiro (Spa-Ant)
2 Castro Marim - Portimao
Candido Barbosa (Por-Lap)
3 Lagoa - Lagos
Martin Garrido Mayorga (Arg-Bar)
4 Vila Real San Antonio -Tavira
Lance Armstrong (Usa-Usp)
5 Parc das Cidades - Malhao
Floyd Landis (Usa-Usp)

FINAL CLASSIFICATION
1 Floyd Landis (Usa-Usp)
2 Victor H.Peña Grisales (Col-Usp)
3 Candido Barbosa (Por-Lap)

21.02: Tour du Haut Var-Fra-180 kms 1.2
Marc Lotz (Ned-Rab)

22.02: Trofeo Luis Puig-Spa-197,3 kms 1.2
Oscar Freire Gomez (Spa-Rab)

22.02: Classico Haribo-Fra-204 kms 1.3
Thor Hushovd (Nor-C.A)

24-27.02: Giro della Provincia di Lucca-Ita-2.3
1 Viareggio - Capannori
Alessandro Petacchi (Ita-Fas)
2 Massarosa - Lido di Camaiore
Alessandro Petacchi (Ita-Fas)
3 Lucca - Castelvecchio Pascoli
Alessandro Bertolini (Ita-Alb)
4 Castelnuovo di Garfagnana-Altopascio
Florent Brard (Fra-Cho)

FINAL CLASSIFICATION
1 Alessandro Bertolini (Ita-Alb)
2 Thomas Ziegler (Ger-Gst)
3 Matteo Tosatto (Ita-Fas)

24-28.02: Volta a la Comunitat Valenciana - Spa - 2.3
1 Xabea - Xabea
Antonio Colom Mas (Spa-Ibb)
2 Xabea - Calp
Alejandro Valverde Belmonte (Spa-Kel)
3 Calp - Port de Sagunt
Alejandro Valverde Belmonte (Spa-Kel)
4 Sagunt - Alt del Campello (Vallada)
Jorge Garcia Marin (Spa-Baq)
5 Valencia -Valencia
Alexandre Usov (Blr-Pho)

FINAL CLASSIFICATION
1 Alejandro Valverde Belmonte (Spa-Kel)
2 Antonio Colom Mas (Spa-Ibb)
3 David Blanco Rodriguez (Spa-Kel)

27.03: GP E3-Harelbeke-Bel-202 km 1.1
Tom Boonen (Bel-Qsd)

28.02: GP Citta Di Chiasso-Swi-165,7 km 1.3
Franco Pellizotti (Ita-Alb)

29.02: Kuurne-Brussels-Kuurne-Bel-193km 1.2
Steven de Jongh (Ned-Rab)

29.02: Giro di Lugano-Swi-160km 1.3
Frédéric Bessy (Fra-Cof)

29.02: Clasica de Almeria-Spa-187km 1.3
Jérôme Pineau (Fra-Blb)

03.03: Mem.Samyn-Fayt-le-Franc-Bel-190km 1.3
Robbie McEwen (Aus-Lot)

03-07.03: Vuelta a Murcia-Spa- 2.3
1 Murcia - San Pedro del Pinatar
Max van Heeswijk (Ned-Usp)
2 Lorca - Lorca
José I.Gutierrez Palacios (Spa-Ibb)
3 Yecla - Yecla
Max van Heeswijk (Ned-Usp)
4 Totana - Collado Bermejo
Danilo Di Luca (Ita-Sae)
5 Murcia - Murcia
Luciano Pagliarini Mendonca (Bra-Lam)

FINAL CLASSIFICATION
1 Alejandro Valverde Belmonte (Spa-Kel)
2 José I. Gutierrez Palacios (Spa-Ibb)
3 Cadel Evans (Aus-Mob)

05-07.03: 3 Daagse van West Vlaanderen 2.3
1 Bellegem
Robert Bartko (Ger-Rab)
2 Handzame-Koksijde-Handzame
Jaan Kirsipuu (Est-A2r)
3 Ichtegem - Ichtegem
Jaan Kirsipuu (Est-A2r)

FINAL CLASSIFICATION
Robert Bartko (Ger-Rab)
Jaan Kirsipuu (Est-A2r)
Kurt-Asle Arvesen (Nor-Csc)

06.03: Giro Prov. di Reggio Calabria-Ita-184 km 1.3
Andris Nauduzs (Lat-Dve)

08.03: Trofeo dell'Etna-Ita-195 km 1.3
Leonardo Bertagnolli (Ita-Sae)
17.03: Nokere-Koerse-Bel- 193 km- 1.3
Max van Heeswijk (Ned-Usp)

21.03: Cholet-Pays De Loire-Fra- 202kms 1.2
Bert De Waele (Bel-Lan)

21.03: Grote Prijs Rudy Dhaenens-Bel -191km 1.3
Geert Omloop (Bel-Mrb)

21.03:Stausee Rundfahrt-Swi-188 km 1.3
Andris Nauduzs (Lat-Dve)

22-26.03: Setmana Catalana de Ciclisme-Spa-2.1
1 Lloret de Mar-Lloret de Mar
Fabian Cancellara (Swi-Fas)
2 Lloret de Mar-Empúriabrava
Beat Zberg (Swi-Gst)
3 Castelló D'Empúries-Montcada I Reixac
Isaac Galvez Lopez (Spa-Ibb)
4 Instalaciones Würth - Port del Comte
Levi Leipheimer (Usa-Rab)
5 Solsona - Parets del Vallès
Angel Edo Alsina (Spa-Mil)

FINAL CLASSIFICATION
1 Joaquin Rodriguez Oliver (Spa-Sdv)
2 Miguel Martín Perdiguero (Spa-Sdv)
3 Josep Jufre Pou (Spa-Reb)

24.03: Dwars door Vlaanderen Waregem -Bel-204 km 1.2
Ludovic Capelle (Bel-Lan)

Geert Omloop

24-28.03: Settimana Internazionale di Coppi & Bartali-Ita 2.3
1a Riccione-Riccione
Graziano Gasparre (Ita-Den)
1b Misano-Misano
Marco Velo (Ita-Fas)
2 Riccione-Faenza
Mirko Celestino (Ita-Sae)
3 Emilia-Scandiano
Crescenzo D'Amore (Ita-A&S)
4 Casalgrande-Pavullo
Michele Scarponi (Ita-Dve)
5 Castellarano-Sassuolo
Ruggero Marzoli (Ita-A&S)

FINAL CLASSIFICATION
1 Giuliano Figueras (Ita-Pan)
2 Mirko Celestino (Ita-Sae)
3 Michele Scarponi (Ita-Dve)

27-28.03: Critérium International-Fra- 2.1
1 Rethel-Charleville-Mézières
Jean-Patrick Nazon (Fra-A2r)
2 Les Mazures - Monthermé
Jens Voigt (Ger-Csc)
3 Charleville-Mézières
Jens Voigt (Ger-Csc)

FINAL CLASSIFICATION
1 Jens Voigt (Ger-Csc)
2 José I.Gutierrez Palacios (Spa-Ibb)
3 Lance Armstrong (Usa-Usp)

28.03: Brabantse Pijl-Bel-194 km 1.2
Luca Paolini (Ita-Qsd)

30.03-01.04: Driedaagse van de Panne-Koksijde-Bel- 2.2
1 Middelkerke-Zottegem
Danilo Hondo (Ger-Gst)
2 Zottegem-Koksijde-Oostduinkerke
Baden Cooke (Aus-FdJ)
3 De Panne-De Panne
Marco Zanotti (Ita-Vin)
4 De Panne
Laszlo Bodrogi (Hun-Qsd)

FINAL CLASSIFICATION
1 George Hincapie (Usa-Usp)
2 Danilo Hondo (Ger-Gst)
3 Gerben Löwik (Ned-Cho)

02.04: Route Adélie de Vitré-Fra-185,3kms 1.3
Anthony Geslin (Fra-Blb)

03.04: G.P. Miguel Indurain-Spa-189kms 1.2
Matthias Kessler (Ger-Tmo)
04.04: G.P. Rennes-Fra- 1.3
Andrus Aug (Est-Dve)

06-09.04: Circuit de la Sarthe-Fra- 2.3
1 Saint Jean De Monts-Vallet

Franck Bouyer (Fra-Blb)
2 Vallet-Montreuil-Juigne
Ludovic Turpin (Fra-A2r)
3 Montreuil-Juigne-Evron
Laurent Brochard (Fra-A2r)
4 Evron-Le Mans
Tomas Lövkvist (Swe-FdJ)

FINAL CLASSIFICATION
1 Tomas Lövqvist (Swe-FdJ)
2 Franck Bouyer (Fra-Blb)
3 Ronny Scholz (Ger-Gst)

08.04: GP Pino Cerami-Wasmuel-Bel 193,1km 1.3
Nico Sijmens (Bel-Lan)

10.04: Ronde van Drente-Ned- 202kms 1.3
Erik Dekker (Ned-Rab)

11.04: G.P. Primavera Amorebieta-Spa 182kms 1.3
Alejandro Valverde Belmonte (Spa-Kel)

12.04: Rund um Köln-Ger-201,2km 1.2
Erik Zabel (Ger-Tmo)

13.04: Paris-Camembert Lepetit-Fra- 1.2
Franck Bouyer (Fra-Blb)

Alexander Vinokourov

13-18.04: Volta do Rio de Janeiro-Bra 2.3
prologue Praia do Leme
Marcos Novello (Bra)
1 Niterói - Cabo Frio
Jorge Giacinti (Arg)
2 Cabo Frio - Cabo Frio
Marcio May (Bra)
3 Conceição de Macabu - Nova Friburgo
Mattej Murgeli (Slo)
4 Nova Friburgo - Niterói
Mattej Murgerli (Slo)
5 Niteroi/Rio de Janeiro
Gil Cordoves (Cub)

FINAL CLASSIFICATION
1 Marcio May (Bra)
2 Luiz Amorim (Bra)
3 Breno Sidoti (Bra)

14.04: Grote Scheldeprijs-Bel-200 km 1.1
Tom Boonen (Bel-Qsd)

14-18.04: Vuelta Ciclista a Aragon- 2.2
1 Teruel-Estacion de Esqui de Valdelinares
Denis Menchov (Rus-Ibb)
2 Calandra - Barbastro
Alessandro Petacchi (Ita-Fas)
3 Sabiñánigo - Sabiñánigo
Constantino Zaballa Gutierrez (Spa-Sdv)
4 Huesca - La Muela
Oscar Laguna Garcia (Spa-Reb)
5 Colchón Relax (La Muela)-Zaragoza
Alessandro Petacchi (Ita-Fas)

FINAL CLASSIFICATION
1 Stefano Garzelli (Ita-Vin)
2 Denis Menchov (Rus-Ibb)
3 Leonardo Piepoli (Ita-Sdv)

15.04: G.P. Denain-Fra-201,4 km 1.3
Thor Hushovd (Nor-C.A)

16.04: Veenendaal-Veenendaal-Ned 207,4 km 1.2
Simone Cadamuro (Ita-Den)

17.04: Groningen-Münster-Ger-201,5 km 1.3
Robert Förster (Ger-Gst)

17.04: Omloop Wase Scheldeboorden-Bazel-Kruibeke-Bel-182 km 1.3
Stefan van Dijk (Ned-Lot)

18.04: Tour de Vendée-Fra-193 km 1.3
Thor Hushovd (Nor-C.A)

20-23.04: Giro del Trentino-Ita 2.2
1 Arco-Marcena di Ruomo
Damiano Cunego (Ita-Sae)
2 Livo di Val di Non-Roncone
Damiano Cunego (Ita-Sae)
3 Breguzzo - Fiavè
Juan M.Mercado Martin (Spa-Qsd)
4 Terme di Comano- Arco
Jan Svorada (Cze-Lam)

FINAL CLASSIFICATION
1 Damiano Cunego (Ita-Sae)
2 Jure Golcer (Slo-Fpf)
3 Gilberto Simoni (Ita-Sae)

Angel Edo Alsina (Spa-Mil)
2 Mr Cortez / Mafra
Carlos Torrent Tarres (Spa-Alm)
3 Circuito Mr Cortez
Pedro Cardoso (Por-Mil)
4 Portela De Sintra / Agualva-Cacém
Pedro Cardoso (Por-Mil)

FINAL CLASSIFICATION
1 Angel Edo Alsina (Spa-Mil)
2 Pedro M. Lopes Goncalves (Por-Lap)
3 Pedro Cardoso (Por-Mil)

23-25.04: Vuelta Ciclista a la Rioja 2.3
1 Autol - Calahorra
Jan Kuyckx (Bel-Vla)
2 Lardero - Est.Esqui Valdezcaray
Jonathan Gonzalez Rios (Spa-Alm)
3 Parque Rioja - Logroño
Jan Kuyckx (Bel-Vla)

FINAL CLASSIFICATION
1 Vladimir Karpets (Rus-Ibb)
2 José A. Gomez Marchante (Spa-Alm)
3 Josep Jufre Pou (Spa-Reb)

25.04: Giro dell'Appennino-Ita- 1.2
Damiano Cunego (Ita-Sae)

01.05: Rund um den Henninger Turm-Frankfurt-Ger 1.1
Karsten Kroon (Ned-Rab)

01.05: GP Industria & Artigianato-Larciano-Ita 1.2
Damiano Cunego (Ita-Sae)

01.05: GP SATS-Midtbank-Den-199 km 1.3
Frank Høj (Den-Csc)

02.05: Giro di Toscana-Ita-170 km 1.3
Matteo Tosatto (Ita-Fas)

02.05: GP Krka - Slo - cat. 1.3
Uros Murn (Slo-Pho)

02.05: Trophée des Grimpeurs-Poly-multipliée-Fra 1.3
Christophe Moreau (Fra-C.A)

05-09.05: 4 Jours de Dunkerque-Fra 2.1
1 Dunkerque-Steenvoorde
Jimmy Casper (Fra-Cof)
2 Hem-Saint Pol sur Mer
Marc Streel (Bel-Lan)
3 Hondshoote-Longuenesse
Didier Rous (Fra-Blb)

20-25.04: Tour of Georia-Usa 2.3
1 Macon - Macon
Gordon Fraser (Can-Hnc)
2 Thomaston - Columbus
Mario Cipollini (Ita-Dve)
3 Carrollton - Rome
Lance Armstrong (Usa-Usp)
4 Rome - Ind.Time Trial
Lance Armstrong (Usa-Usp)
5 Dalton - Dahlonega
Jason McCartney (Usa-Hnc)
6 Athens - Hiawassee
Cesar A.Grajales Calle (Col-Jit)
7 Dawsonville - Alpharetta
Gordon Fraser (Can-Hnc)

FINAL CLASSIFICATION
1 Lance Armstrong (Usa-Usp)
2 Jens Voigt (Ger-Csc)
3 Chris Horner (Usa-Web)

21-25.04: Niedersachsen Rundfahrt-Ger- 2.3
1 Wolfsburg – Duderstadt
Danilo Hondo (Ger-Gst)
2 Duderstadt – Göttingen
Danilo Hondo (Ger-Gst)
3 Göttingen – Einbeck
Bert Roesems (Bel-Reb)
4 Einbeck – Melle
Danilo Hondo (Ger-Gst)
5 Melle - Leer
Danilo Hondo (Ger-Gst)

FINAL CLASSIFICATION
1 Bert Roesems (Bel-Reb)
2 Stefan Kupfernagel (Ger-Tlm)
3 Stephan Schreck (Ger-Tmo)

22-25.04 GP Internacional MR Cortez-Mitsubishi-Por- 2.3
1 Torres Vedras / Torres Vedras

25.04: Ronde van Noord Holland- Ned 200 km 1.3
Stefan van Dijk (Ned-Lot)

25.04: Tro-Bro Leon-Fra-195,2 km 1.3
Samuel Dumoulin (Fra-A2r)

28.04-02.05: Vuelta a Castilla-Leon-Spa 2.3
1 Belorado - Castrojeriz
José I.Gutierrez Palacios (Spa-Ibb)
2 Frómista- Carrión de los Condes TTT:
Illes Balears-Banesto
3 Carrión de los Condes-Mansilla de las Mulas
Alejandro Valverde Belmonte (Spa-Kel)
4 León - Ponferrada
Alejandro Valverde Belmonte (Spa-Kel)
5 Ponferrada - Villafranca del Bierzo
Alejandro Valverde Belmonte (Spa-Kel)

FINAL CLASSIFICATION
1 Koldo Gil Perez (Spa-Lst)
2 David Navas Chica (Spa-Ibb)
3 José I.Gutierrez Palacios (Spa-Ibb)

4 Neufchatel Hardelot-Boulogne sur Mer
Stijn Devolder (Bel-Usp)
5 Dunkerque (Place Charles Valentin)
Danilo Hondo (Ger-Gst)
6 Dunkerque - Dunkerque
Max van Heeswijk (Ned-Usp)
Final Ranking
1 Sylvain Chavanel (Fra-Blb)
2 Laurent Brochard (Fra-A2r)
3 Didier Rous (Fra-Blb)

08-09.05: Classica de Alcobendas 2.3
1 Alcobendas - Puerto de Navacerrada
Iban Mayo Diez (Spa-Eus)
2 Collado Villalba - Collado Villalba
Iban Mayo Diez (Spa-Eus)
3 Alcobendas - Alcobendas
Luis Leon Sanchez Gil (Spa-Lst)

FINAL CLASSIFICATION
1 Iban Mayo Diez (Spa-Eus)
2 Eladio Jiménez Sanchez (Spa-Kel)
3 David Moncoutié (Fra-Cof)

Johan Museeuw

08-16.05: 57th Friedensfahrt/Závod míru/Wyscig Pokoju 2.2
1 Rund um Brüssel (Bel)
Lars Wackernagel (Ger-Wie)
2 Rund um Hannover (Ger)
Denis Bertolini (Ita-A&S)
3 Hemmingen - Halberstadt (Ger)
Sebastian Siedler (Ger-Wie)
4 Eisleben - Beierfeld (Ger)
Michele Scarponi (Ita-Dve)
5 Görlitz - Wroclaw (Pol)
Martin Hvastija (Slo-Alb)
6 Szczawno Zdroj - Jelenia Gora (Pol)
Slawomir Kohut (Pol-Hop)
7 Szklarska Poreba -Teplice (Cze)
Erik Zabel (Ger-Tmo)
8 Bilina - Karlovy Vary (Cze)
David Loosli (Swi-Sae)
9 Karlovy Vary - Praha (Cze)
Erik Zabel (Ger-Tmo)

FINAL CLASSIFICATION
1 Michele Scarponi (Ita-Dve)
2 Slawomir Kohut (Pol-Hop)
3 Roger Beuchat (Swi-Vin)

11.05: Subida al Naranco-Spa-162 kms 1.3
Iban Mayo Diez (Spa-Eus)
12-16.05: Vuelta Ciclista Asturias-Spa 2.2
1 Oviedo - Llanes
Luis L.Sanchez Gil (Spa-Lst)
2 Llanes - Gijon
David Herrero Llorente (Spa-Alm)
3 Gijon - Avilés
Carlos Barredo Llamazales (Spa-Lst)
4 Cafés Toscaf - Santuario del Acebo
Jonathan Gonzalez Rios (Spa-Alm)
5 Cangas del Narcea - Oviedo
Miguel A.Martin Perdiguero (Spa-Sdv)

FINAL CLASSIFICATION
1 Iban Mayo Diez (Spa-Eus)
2 Félix Cárdenas Ravalo (Col-Baq)
3 Haimar Zubeldia Agirre (Spa-Eus)

14-16.05: Tour de Picardie-Fra 2.2
1 Hirson - Doullens
Tom Boonen (Bel-Qsd)
2 Crécy-en-Ponthieu - Compiègne
Tom Boonen (Bel-Qsd)
3 La Croix-Saint-Ouen - Soissons

Stefan van Dijk (Ned-Lot)
4 Soissons - Chauny
Jimmy Casper (Fra-Cof)

FINAL CLASSIFICATION
1 Tom Boonen (Bel-Qsd)
2 Jimmy Casper (Fra-Cof)
3 Stefan van Dijk (Ned-Lot)

16.05: Rund um den Flughafen Köln-Bonn-Ger-205km 1.3
Pascal Hungerbühler (Swi-Vol)

19-23.05: Tour du Languedoc-Roussillon-Fra 2.1
1 Maury - Port-Vendres
Thor Hushovd (Nor-C.A)
2 Port-Leucate - Narbonne
Thor Hushovd (Nor-C.A)
3 Ganges - Aigues-Mortes
Martin Elmiger (Swi-Pho)
4 Pont du Gard - Mende
Christophe Moreau (Fra-C.A)
5 Florac - Sète
Lance Armstrong (Usa-Usp)

FINAL CLASSIFICATION
1 Christophe Moreau (Fra-C.A)
2 Viatcheslav Ekimov (Rus-Usp)
3 Iker Flores Galarza (Spa-Eus)

19-23.05: Ronde van België/Tour de Belgique-Bel 2.2
1 Oostende - Oostende
Gianluca Bortolami (Ita-Lam)
2 Oostende - Knokke-Heist
Tom Boonen (Bel-Qsd)
3 Knokke-Heist - Buggenhout
Max van Heeswijk (Ned-Usp)
4 Mechelen
Bert Roesems (Bel-Reb)
5 Mechelen - Mechelen
- cancelled -
6 Ans - Eupen
Björn Leukemans (Bel-Mrb)

FINAL CLASSIFICATION
1 Sylvain Chavanel (Fra-Blb)
2 Bart Voskamp (Ned-Cho)
3 Max van Heeswijk (Ned-Usp)

19-23.05: Internationale Bayern Rundfahrt-Ger- 2.3
1 Selb - Roth
Antonio Bucciero (Ita-Sae)
2 Roth - Aichach
Erik Zabel (Ger-Tmo)
3 Aichach
Michael Rich (Ger-Gst)
4 München - Bad Aibling
Massimiliano Gentili (Ita-Dve)
5 Bad Aibling - Pfarrkirchen
Erik Zabel (Ger-Tmo)
6 Pfarrkirchen – Burghausen
Stefan Schuhmacher (Ger-Tlm)

FINAL CLASSIFICATION
1 Jens Voigt (Ger-Csc)
2 Andreas Klöden (Ger-Tmo)
3 Tomasz Brozyna (Pol-Ati)

26-30.05: Volta ao Alentejo-Por- 2.3
1 Beja - Beja
Alberto Benito Guerreiro (Spa-Ant)
2 Viana do Alentejo - Mora
Hugo Sabido (Por-Mil)
3 Alter do Chão - Portalegre
Daniel Petrov (Bul-Cab)
4 Estremoz - Elvas
Krassimir Vasilev (Bul-Wbp)
5 Redondo - Adega Cooperativa de Redondo
Joaquim C.Sampaio (Por-Cab)

FINAL CLASSIFICATION
1 Daniel Petrov (Bul-Cab)
2 Joaquim Andrade (Por-Wbp)
3 Joaquim C.Sampaio (Por-Cab)

27-30.05: Tour de Luxembourg-Lux 2.2
1 Luxembourg - Mondorf
Lars Ytting Bak (Den-Bgl)
2 Wasserbillig - Leudelange
Tom Steels (Bel-Lan)
3 Mersch - Luxembourg
Maxime Monfort (Bel-Lan)
4 Bettembourg - Bettembourg
Fabian Cancellara (Swi-Fas)
5 Wiltz - Diekirch
Kim Kirchen (Lux-Fas)

FINAL CLASSIFICATION
1 Maxime Monfort (Bel-Lan)
2 Torsten Hiekmann (Ger-Tmo)
3 Jörg Jaksche (Ger-Csc)

28.05: Baltic Open-Tallinn GP-Est-180km 1.3
Mark Scanlon (Irl-A2r)

29.05: Ühispanga Tartu Tänavasoít -Est-187,5 km 1.3
Mark Scanlon (Irl-A2r)

29.05: A Travers le Morbihan-Fra-181km 1.3
Thomas Voeckler (Fra-Blb)

30.05: GP Llodio-Spa-175,5 km 1.3
Unai Etxebarria Arana (Ven-Eus)

31.05: Prix de la Ville Cotterets-Fra- 1.3
Stuart O'Grady (Aus-Cof)

31.05-06.06: Deutschland-Tour-Ger- 2.2
1 Time Trial in Karlsruhe
Michael Rich (Ger-Gst)
2 Bad Urach - Wangen/Allgäu
Tom Boonen (Bel-Qsd)
3 Wangen/Allgäu - St. Anton/Arlberg (Aut)
Patrik Sinkewitz (Ger-Qsd)
4 Bad Tölz - Landshut
Sébastien Hinault (Fra-C.A)
5 Kelheim - Kulmbach
Allan Davis (Aus-Lst)
6 Kulmbach-Fichtelberg/Oberwiesenthen
Francisco Mancebo Perez (Spa-Ibb)
7 Chemnitz - Leipzig
Tom Boonen (Bel-Qsd)

FINAL CLASSIFICATION
1 Patrik Sinkewitz (Ger-Qsd)
2 Jens Voigt (Ger-Csc)
3 Jan Hruska (Cze-Lst)

01.06: Wachovia International-Usa-147km 1.3
Max van Heeswijk (Ned-Usp)

02-06.06: Euskal Bizikleta-Bicicleta Vasca -Spa- 2.1
1 Eibar - Karrantza
Miguel A.Martin Perdiguero (Spa-Sdv)
2 Karrantza - Agurain
Miguel A.Martin Perdiguero (Spa-Sdv)
3 Agurain - Bidegoian
Angel Vicioso Arcos (Spa-Lst)
4a Bidegoian - Abadiño
Dmitri Konyshev (Rus-Lpr)
4b Elorrio - Abadiño
Angel Vicioso Arcos (Spa-Lst)
5 Abadiño - Arrate (Eibar)
Roberto Laiseka Jaio (Spa-Eus)

FINAL CLASSIFICATION
1 Roberto Heras Hernandez (Spa-Lst)
2 Roberto Laiseka Jaio (Spa-Eus)
3 Samuel Sanchez Gonzalez (Spa-Eus)

03.06: Wachovia Classic-Usa-147 km 1.3
Fred Rodriguez (Usa-A&S)

05.06: Classique des Alpes-Fra-165 km 1.1
Oscar Pereiro Sio (Spa-Pho)

06.06: Wachovia USPro-Champ.-Usa-250km 1.2
Francisco Ventoso Alberdi (Spa-Sdv)

07-13.06: Osterreich Rundfahrt-Aut 2.2
1 Salzburg - Salzburg
Tom Steels (Bel-Lan)
2 Salzburg - Kitzbüheler Horn
Cadel Evans (Aus-Tmo)
3 Kitzbühel - Bad Hofgastein
Tom Steels (Bel-Lan)
4 Bad Gastein - Lienz / Tristacher See-Gerrit Glomser (Aut-Sae)
5 Lienz - St. Veit an der Glan
Filippo Simeoni (Ita-Dve)
6 St. Veit an der Glan-Bad Radkersburg
Jan Kuyckx (Bel-Vla)
7 Wien, Ringstraße
Ludo Dierckxens (Bel-Lan)

FINAL CLASSIFICATION
1 Cadel Evans (Aus-Tmo)
2 Michele Scarponi (Ita-Dve)
3 Maurizio Vandelli (Ita-Rad)

15-20.06: Grand Prix Cycliste de Beauce -Can-2.3
1 Québec
Ivan Dominguez (Cub-Cob)
2 Saint-Joseph - Saint-Joseph
Tomasz Brozyna (Pol-Ati)
3 Lac-Etchemin - Lac-Etchemin
Charles Dionne (Can-Web)
4 Saint-Georges - Mt. Mégantic
Radoslaw Romanik (Pol-Hop)
5a Québec: Notre-Dame-des-Pins
Nathan O'Neill (Aus-Cob)
5b Saint-Georges
Ciaran Power (Irl-Nic)
6 urban circuit thru Saint-Georges
Aaron Olson (Usa-Cob)

FINAL CLASSIFICATION
1 Tomasz Brozyna (Pol-Ati)
2 Nathan O'Neill (Aus-Cob)
3 Scott Moninger (Usa-Hnc)

16-20.06: STER Electrotour-Ned- 2.3
1 Veldhoven = prologue
Tom Boonen (Bel-Qsd)
2 Eindhoven-Nuth
Tom Boonen (Bel-Qsd)
3 Valkenburg-Walkenburg
Preben Van Hecke (Bel-Reb)
4 Coo-La Gileppe (Jalhay)
Nick Nuyens (Bel-Qsd)
5 Sittard/Geleen-Schijndel
Niko Eeckhout (Bel-Lot)

FINAL CLASSIFICATION
1 Nick Nuyens (Bel-Qsd)
2 Paul Van Hyfte (Bel-Vla)
3 Philippe Gilbert (Bel-FdJ)

19-22.06: Route du Sud-Fra- 2.3
1 Castres - Vielha (Spa)
Cristian Moreni (Ita-Alb)
2 Les (Spa) - St.Gaudens
Francis Mourey (Fra-FdJ)
3 Loures Barousse - Champ

Bradley McGee (Aus-FdJ)
4 Montrejeau-Loudienvielle Le Louron
Thomas Voeckler (Fra-Blb)

FINAL CLASSIFICATION
1 Bradley McGee (Aus-FdJ)
2 Sandy Casar (Fra-FdJ)
3 Torsten Hiekmann (Ger-Tmo)

23.06: Noord Nederland Tour-Ned- 1.3
Tom Veelers (Ned-Lmt)

30.06-04.07: Course de la Solidarité Olympique-Pol 2.3
1 Lódz - Kielce
Dariusz Rudnicki (Pol-Leg)
2 Jedrzejów - Sandomierz
Robert Radosz (Psb)
3 Ozarów
Bogdan Bondariew (Ukr-Ati)
4 Krasnik - Mielec
Krzysztof Jezowski (Pol-Mik)
5 Bochnia - Bielsko-Biala
Jonas Holmkvist (Swe-Tbn)
6 Rybnik - Rybnik
Marcin Gebka (Pol-Dhl)

FINAL CLASSIFICATION
1 Bogdan Bondariew (Ukr-Ati)
2 Slawomir Kohut (Pol-Hop)
3 Piotr Mazur (Pol-Mos)

03.07: Criterium d'Abruzzo-Ita-171,8km 1.3
Enrico Degano (Ita-Team Barloworld)

04.07: Trofeo Matteotti-Ita-188,5 km- 1.2
Danilo Di Luca (Ita-Sae)

04.07: Tour du Doubs-Fra-190,5 km- 1.3
Matthieu Sprick (Fra-Blb)

07-10.07: Int. UNIQA Classic-Aut- 2.3
1 Traismauer - Traismauer
Robert Hunter (Rsa-Rab)
2 Traismauer - Rabenstein
Kjell Carlström (Fin-Amo)
3 Rabenstein - Gresten
Robert Hunter (Rsa-Rab)
4 Gresten - Waidhofen a.d. Ybbs
Pedro Horrillo Munoz (Spa-Qsd)

FINAL CLASSIFICATION
1 Kjell Carlström (Fin-Amo)
2 Mikhail Timochine (Rus-Lan)
3 Matej Jurco (Svk-Den)

07-11.07: GP Joaquim Agostinho/ T.Vedras -Por- 2.3
1 Silveira - Torres Vedras
Daniel Petrov (Bul-Cab)
2 Azambuja - Lourinha
Angel Edo Alsina (Spa-Mil)
3 S.M.Agraço - Alto Montejunto
Alexis Rodriguez Hernandez (Spa-Bep)
4 Praia Da Areia Branco - Lisboa Alberto Benito Guerreiro (Spa-Ant)
5 Circuito Torres Vedras
Ruben Plaza Molina (Spa-Kel)

FINAL CLASSIFICATION
1 David Bernabeu Armengol (Spa-Mil)
2 Nelson Vitorino (Por-Wbp)
3 Daniel Petrov (Bul-Cab)

17.07: GP Citta Rio Saliceto-Corregio-Ita-160,4km 1.3
Przemyslaw Niemec (Pol-Mie)

17-25.07: Tour of Qinghai Lake -Chn- 2.3
1 Xining Circuit
Viktor Rapinski (Blr-Nic)
2 Xining-Xihaizhen
Jeff Louder (Usa-Nic)
3 Xihaizhen-Niaodao(Bird Island)Simone Cadamuro (Ita-Den)
4 Niaodao-Qinghai Lake Hotel
Viktor Rapinski (Blr-Nic)
5 Qinghai Lake Hotel-Xining
Jeremy Maartens (Rsa-*El.2)
6 Xining-Menyuan
Marco Fertonani (Ita-Pho)
7 Menyuan-Huzhu
Andrei Mizourov (Kaz-Okt)
8 Xining-Ledu-Pingan-Xining
André Schulze (Ger-Vcf)
9 Xining Circuit
Viktor Rapinski (Blr-Nic)

FINAL CLASSIFICATION
1 Phillip Zajicek (Usa-Nic)
2 Ryan Cox (Rsa-Tbl)
3 Ghader Mizbani Iranagh (Iri-Gnt)

21-25.07: Sachsen-Tour International-Ger- 2.3
1 Dresden - Zittau
Stephan Schreck (Ger-Tmo)
2 Zittau - Leipzig
Olaf Pollack (Ger-Gst)
3 Leipzig - Klingenthal

Davide Rebellin (Ita-Gst)
4a Rittersgrün-Kurort Oberwiesenthal/Fichtelberg
Davide Rebellin(Ita-Gst)
4b Kurort Oberwiesenthal-Freital
Robert Hunter (Rsa-Rab)
5 Dresden – Dresden
Björn Schröder (Ger-Wie)

FINAL CLASSIFICATION
1 Andrey Kashechkin (Kaz-C.A)
2 Tomas Konecny (Cze-Tmo)
3 Christian Pfannberger (Aut-Zvz)

23-25.07: Brixia Tour -Ita- 2.3
1 San Vigilio di Concesio-Toscolano Maderno
Igor Astarloa Askasibar (Spa-Lam)
2 Darfo Boario Terme-Valpalot di Pisogne
Julio Alb.Perez Cuapio (Mex-Pan)
3 Pisogne - Darfo Boario Terme
Yuri Mitlushenko (Ukr-Lan)
4 Bettole di Buffalora-Manerbio
Enrico Degano (Ita-Tbl)

FINAL CLASSIFICATION
1 Danilo Di Luca (Ita-Sae)
2 Paolo Tiralongo (Ita-Pan)
3 Massimiliano Gentili (Ita-Dve)

25.07: GP Villafranca de Ordizia-Spa-156km 1.2
David Herrero Llorente (Spa-Alm)

26-30.07: Tour de la Région Wallone-Bel- 2.3
1 Aubel - Bassenge
Hayden Roulston (NZl-Cof)
2 Amay - Arlon
Fabrizio Guidi (Ita-Csc)
3 Ardenne - Nijvel
Nicolas Reynaud (Fra-Rag)
4 Jodoigne - Bruxelles
Jaan Kirsipuu (Est-A2r)
5 Bruxelles - Charleroi
Sébastien Chavanel (Fra-Blb)

FINAL CLASSIFICATION
1 Gerben Löwik (Ned-Cho)
2 Bert De Waele (Bel-Lan)
3 Christophe Agnolutto (Fra-A2r)

29.07-08.08: Volta a Portugal-Por- 2.2
1 Termas de Monfortinho - Castelo Branco
José M.Elías Galindo (Spa-Reb)
2 Castelo Branco - Cartaxo
Candido Barbosa (Por-Lap)
3 Batalha (Fassa Bortolo) - Viseu
Jose Cayetano Julia Cegarra (Spa-Kel)
4 Viseu - Senhora da Graça
David Arroyo Duran (Spa-Lap)
5 Santo Tirso - Fafe
Adolfo García Quesada (Spa-Kel)
6 Fafe - Santa Maria da Feira
Fabio Sacchi (Ita-Fas)
7 S. João de Madeira - Gouveia Sergio Paulinho (Por-Lap)
8 Fundão - Torre
David Arroyo Duran (Spa-Lap)
9 Figueira da Foz - Alcobaça
Alberto Ongarato (Ita-Fas)
10 Oeiras - Sintra
Sergio Paulinho (Por-Lap)

FINAL CLASSIFICATION
1 David Bernabeu Armengol (Spa-Mil)
2 David Arroyo Duran (Spa-Lap)
3 Nuno Ribeiro (Por-Lap)

31.07: LUK Cup-Duo-Time Trial-Ger 1.2
Team CSC: Bobby Julich (Usa)-Jens Voigt (Ger)

31.07: Circuito de Getxo-Memor. Ricardo Otxoa-Spa-185 km 1.3
Gert VanderAerden (Bel-MrB)

01.08: Polynormande-Fra- 1.3
Sylvain Chavanel (Fra-Blb)

02-05.08: Vuelta Ciclista a Burgos-Spa- 2.1
1 Burgos - Poza De La Sal (Altotero)
Alejandro Valverde Belmonte (Spa-Kel)
2 Lerma - Aranda de Duero
Alejandro Valverde Belmonte (Spa-Kel)
3 Areniscas De Los Pinares-Lagunas de Neila
Alejandro Valverde Belmonte (Spa-Kel)
4 Miranda de Ebro-Burgos
Aurélien Clerc (Swi-Qsd)

FINAL CLASSIFICATION
1 Alejandro Valverde Belmonte (Spa-Kel)
2 Denis Menchov (Rus-Ibb)
3 Leonardo Piepoli (Ita-Sdv)

04.08: GP Citta di Camaiore-Ita-193 km 1.2
Paolo Bettini (Ita-Qsd)

04-08.08: Post Danmark Rundt-Den- 2.2
1 Aabenraa - Esbjerg
Stuart O'Grady (Aus-Cof)
2 Varde - Århus
Fabrizio Guidi (Ita-Csc)
3 Århus – Vejle
Janek Tombak (Est-Cof)
4 Fredericia
Jens Voigt (Ger-Csc)
5 Odense - Roskilde
Tomas Vaitkus (Ltu-Lan)
6 Tåstrup - Frederiksberg
Jimmy Casper (Fra-Cof)

FINAL CLASSIFICATION
1 Kurt-Asle Arvesen (Nor-Csc)
2 Jens Voigt (Ger-Csc)
3 Stuart O'Grady (Aus-Cof)

04-08.08: Regio Tour International-Ger- 2.3
1 Heitersheim - Wehr/Hochrhein, Schwarzwald
Stephan Schreck (Ger-Tmo)
2 Mühlheim
Alexander Vinokourov (Kaz-Tmo)
3 Neunenburg/Rhein-Guebwiller/Elsass
Alexander Vinokourov (Kaz-Tmo)
4 Emmendingen - Lahr
Steven Caethoven (Bel-Vla)
5 Herbolzheim - Vogtsburg am Kaiserstuhl
Nicolas Vogondy (Fra-FdJ)

FINAL CLASSIFICATION
1 Alexander Vinokourov (Kaz-Tmo)
2 Stephan Schreck (Ger-Tmo)
3 Andrey Kashechkin (Kaz-C.A)

08.08: Subida a Urkiola-Spa-160,6 km 1.3
Leonardo Piepoli (Ita-Sdv)

08.08: Sparkassen Giro Bochum -Ger- 175,2 km 1.3
David Kopp (Ger-Tlm)

10.08: 2 Giorni Marchigiana / GP Fred Mengoni - Ita- 204 km 1.3
Damiano Cunego (Ita-Sae)

10-13.08: Tour de L'Ain -Fra- 2.3
1 Miribel – Bourg en Bresse
Jérôme Pineau (Fra-Blb)
2 Lagnieu – Oyonnax
Antonio Cruz (Usa-Usp)
3a Izernore – Saint Genis Pouilly
Jean-Patrick Nazon (Fra-A2r)
3b Saint Genis Pouilly - Lelex Monts Jura
cancelled (heavy storms)
4 Culoz - Belley
Cédric Vasseur (Fra-Cof)

FINAL CLASSIFICATION
1 Jérôme Pineau (Fra-Blb)
2 Leif Hoste (Bel-Lot)
3 Jurgen Van Goolen (Bel-Qsd)

11.08: 2 Giorni Marchigiana / Tr.Citta di Castelfidardo - Ita- 179 km 1.3
Emanuele Sella (Ita-Pan)

14.08: Memorial Henryka Lasaka -Pol- 165 km 1.3
Robert Radosz (Pol-Psb)

17.08: Tre Valli Varese -Ita- 197,9 km 1.1
Fabian Wegmann (Ger-Gst)

17.08: GP Stad Zottegem - Dr. Tistaert Prijs - Bel- 189 km 1.3
David Kopp (Ger-Tlm)

17-20.08: Tour de Limousin -Fra- 2.3
1 Oradour s/Glane - La Souterraine
Saulius Ruskys (Ltu-Okt)
2 La Souterraine - Magnac Bourg
Pierrick Fedrigo (Fra-C.A)
3 St Yrieix la Perche - St Yrieix la Perche
Didier Rous (Fra-Blb)
4 Treignac – Limoges
Cédric Vasseur (Fra-Cof)

FINAL CLASSIFICATION
1 Pierrick Fedrigo (Fra-C.A)
2 Patrick Calcagni (Swi-Vin)
3 Franck Renier (Fra-Blb)

18.08: Coppa Agostini -Ita- 196,8 km 1.2
Leonardo Bertagnolli (Ita-Sae)

19.08: Coppa Bernocchi -Ita- 199,8 km 1.3
Angelo Furlan (Ita-Alb)

21.08: Giro del Veneto -Ita- 206 km 1.1
Gilberto Simoni (Ita-Sae)

21.08: OZ Tour Beneden-Maas -Ned- 198,2 km 1.3
Jans Koerts (Ned-Cho)

22.08: Dwars door Gendringen -Ned- 197,4km 1.3
Stefan van Dijk (Ned-Lot)

22.08: Châteauroux Clas. De l'Indre -Fra- 1.3
Aliaksandr Kuschynski (Blr-Amo)

22.08: Clasica a los Puertos de Guadarrama -Spa- 146 km 1.3
Jorge Ferrío Luque (Spa-Alm)

22.08: GP Schwarzwald -Ger- 1.3
Markus Fothen (Ger-Gst)

22.08: USPro Criterium Championship - Usa - 100 km 1.3
Jonas Carney (Usa-Jel)

24.08: Druivenkoers-Overijse -Bel- 195,6km 1.3
Stefan Schumacher (Ger-Tlm)

24-27.08: Tour du Poitou Charentes -Fra- 2.3
1 Chateauneuf/Chte - Andilly-les-Marais
Danilo Hondo (Ger-Gst)
2 Andilly-les-Marais - Sauzé-Vaussais
Sandy Casar (Fra-FdJ)
3 Sauzé-Vaussais - Lusignan
Sylvain Chavanel (Fra-Blb)
4 Rouillé - Lusignan
Sylvain Chavanel (Fra-Blb)
5 Lusignan - Chasseneuil-du-Poitou
Ludovic Capelle (Bel-Lan)

FINAL CLASSIFICATION
1 Stéphane Barthe (Fra-Okt)
2 Ronald Mutsaars (Ned-Rab)
3 Jimmy Engoulvent (Fra-Cof)

24-28.08: Ronde van Nederland -Ned- 2.1
1 Oudenbosch - Hoorn
Max van Heeswijk (Ned-Usp)
2 Bolsward - Nijverdal
Max van Heeswijk (Ned-Usp)
3 Kleef (Ger) - Goch (Ger)
Alessandro Petacchi (Ita-Fas)
4 Goch (Ger) - Sittard/Geleen
Viatcheslav Ekimov (Rus-Usp)
5 Düsseldorf (Ger) - Sittard/Geleen
Leon van Bon (Ned-Lot)
6 Sittard/Geleen - Landgraaf
Erik Dekker (Ned-Rab)

FINAL CLASSIFICATION
1 Erik Dekker (Ned-Rab)
2 Viatcheslav Ekimov (Rus-Usp)
3 Marc Wauters (Bel-Rab)

25.08: GP Nobili Rubinetterie-Borgomanero -Ita- 184,8 kms 1. 3
Damiano Cunego (Ita-Sae)

28.08: Tour de Friuli -Ita- 198 km 1.3
Michele Gobbi (Ita-Den)

29.08: GP Kanton-Aargau - Gippingen -Swi- 196 km 1.1
Matteo Tosatto (Ita-Fas)

29.08: GP Eddy Merckx - Bel- 1.2
Thomas Dekker (Ned) - Koen de Kort (Ned) = Rabo TT/III

Ivan Basso

30.08: Boucles de l'Aulne - GP Le Télégramme -Fra- 179,4 km 1.3
Frédéric Finot (Fra-Rag)

Gerrit Glomser

31.08: Schaal Sels-Merksem -Bel- 195km 1.3
Geoffry Demeyere (Bel-Vla)

01-05.09: Internat. Hessen Rundfahrt -Ger- 2.3
1 Kassel - Bad Arolsen
Jnai Yus Kerejeta (Spa-Blb)
2 Gießen - Wiesbaden
Roberto Lochowski (Ger-Wie)
3 Wiesbaden - Lich
Sebastian Lang (Ger-Gst)
4 Dieburg - Darmstadt - Dieburg
Michael Rich (Ger-Gst)
5 Dieburg - Frankfurt am Main
Sebastian Siedler (Ger-Wie)

FINAL CLASSIFICATION
1 Sebastian Lang (Ger-Gst)
2 Stefan Schumacher (Ger-Tlm)
3 Jerôme Pineau (Fra-Blb)

01-05.09: Tour of Britain -GBr- 2.3
1 Manchester - Manchester
Stefano Zanini (Ita-Qsd)
2 Leeds - Sheffield
Mauricio Ardila Cano (Col-Cho)
3 Bakewell - Nottingham
Tom Boonen (Bel-Qsd)
4 Newport - Celtic Manor Resort
Mauricio Ardila Cano (Col-Cho)
5 Westminster circuit (45 laps)-London
Enrico Degano (Ita-Tbl)

FINAL CLASSIFICATION
1 Mauricio Ardila Cano (Col-Cho)
2 Julian Dean (NZl-C.A)
3 Nick Nuyens (Bel-Qsd)

02.09: Trofeo Melinda-Val di Non -Ita- 194km 1.2
Davide Rebellin (Ita-Gst)

04.09: Coppa Placci -Ita- 200 km 1.1
Leonardo Bertagnolli (Ita-Sae)

04.09: DELTA Profronde van Midden Zeeland -Ned- 199 km 1.2
Nico Eeckhout (Bel-Lot)

05.09: Giro di Romagna -Ita- 190,2 km 1.2
Gianluca Bortolami (Ita-Lam)

05.09: G.P. Jef Scherens -Bel- 183 km 1.3
Allan Johansen (Den-Bgl)

06-12.09: Tour de Pologne -Pol- 2.2
1 Gdansk - Gdynia
Fabio Baldato (Ita-Alb)
2 Tczew - Olsztyn
Marcin Sapa (Pol-Mik)
3 Ostróda - Bydgoszcz
Allan Davis (Aus-Lst)
4 Inowroclaw - Kalisz
Fabio Baldato (Ita-Alb)
5 Olesnica - Szklarska Poreba
Rinaldo Nocentini (Ita-A&S)
6 Piechowice - Karpacz
Marek Rutkiewicz (Pol-Ati)
7 Jelenia Góra - Karpacz
Hugo Sabido (Por-Mil)
8 Jelenia Góra - Karpacz, czasówka
Ondrej Sosenka (Cze-A&S)

FINAL CLASSIFICATION
1 Ondrej Sosenka (Cze-A&S)
2 Hugo Sabido (Por-Mil)
3 Franco Pellizotti (Ita-Alb)

08.09: Memorial Van Steenbergen - Aartselaar -Bel- 201 km 1.2
Tom Boonen (Bel-Qsd)

09-10.09: Bohemia Tour -Cze- 2.3
1 Beroun - Hudlice
Lubor Tesar (Cze-Zvz)
2 Beroun - Kolednik
Tomas Buchácek (Cze-Fvt)

FINAL CLASSIFICATION
1 Lubor Tesar (Cze-Zvz)
2 Jan Faltynek (Cze-Psk)
3 Milan Kadlec (Cze-Vin)

11.09: Giro Colline del Chianti Val d'Elsa -Ita- 191,6 km 1.3
Krzystof Szczawinski (Pol-Ict)

11.09: Paris - Bruxelles -Bel- 225 km 1.1
Nick Nuyens (Bel-Qsd)

12.09: GP Fourmies -Fra- 202 km 1.1
Andrey Kashechkin (Kaz-C.A)

12.09: Rund um die Nürneberger Altstadt -Ger- 180 km 1.3
Sebastian Siedler (Ger-Wie)

12.09: T Mobile International (San Francisco) -Usa- 186 km 1.3
Charles Dionne (Can-Web)

15.09: G.P. Wallonie -Bel- 1.2
Nick Nuyens (Bel-Qsd)

15-19.09: Rheinland-Pfalz Rundfahrt -Ger- 2.3
1 Pirmasens - Worms
Luke Roberts (Aus-Com)
2 Worms - Mainz
Thomas Dekker (Ned-Rab)
3 Koblenz – Bad Marienberg
Rolf Aldag (Ger-Tmo)
4 Trier - Saarburg
Torsten Schmidt (Ger-Gst)
5 Kaiserslautern - Pirmasens
Andre Korff (Ger-Tmo)

FINAL CLASSIFICATION
1 Björn Glasner (Ger-Tlm)
2 Mauricio Ardila Cano (Col-Cho)
3 Ronny Scholz (Ger-Gst)

17.09: Kampioenschap van Vlaanderen -Bel- 182,6 km 1.3
Jimmy Casper (Fra-Cof)

19.09: Grand Prix des Nations (Time Trial) -Fra- 55 km 1.1
Michael Rich (Ger-Gst)

19.09: G.P. Isbergues -Fra- 201 km 1.2
Ludovic Capelle (Bel-Lan)

19.09: GP Industria & Commercio Prato -Ita- 177,4 km 1.2
Nick Nuyens (Bel-Qsd)

23.09: Coppa Sabatini -Ita-197,7 km 1.2
Jan Ullrich (Ger-Tmo)

23-26.09: Circuit Franco-Belge -Bel- 2.3
1 Dunkerque - Quiévrain
Paolo Bettini (Ita-Qsd)
2 Estaimpuis - Ploegsteert
Jimmy Casper (Fra-Cof)
3 Maubeuge - Mons
Tom Boonen (Bel-Qsd)
4 Beloeil - Tournai
Tom Boonen (Bel-Qsd)

FINAL CLASSIFICATION
1 Jimmy Casper (Fra-Cof)
2 Steven de Jongh (Ned-Rab)
3 Nico Mattan (Bel-Reb)

24-26.09: Paris-Corrèze -Fra- 2.3
1 Contres - Saint Amand Montrond
Jaan Kirsipuu (Est-A2r)
2 Saint Amand Montrond-Chatel-Guyon
Florent Brard (Fra-Cho)
3 Objat-Objat
Eric Berthou (Fra-Rag)

FINAL CLASSIFICATION
1 Philippe Gilbert (Bel-FdJ)
2 Simon Gerrans (Aus-A2r-stag)
3 Koen de Kort (Ned-Rb3)

25.09: Giro dell'Emilia -Ita- 197 km 1.1
Ivan Basso (Ita-Csc)

26.09: Milano-Vignola (GP Berghelli) -Ita- 199 km 1.2
Danilo Hondo (Ger-Gst)

03.10: Memorial Manuel Galera -Spa- 146 km 1.3
Luis Pasamontes Rodriguez (Spa-Reb)

07.10: Paris-Bourges -Fra- 196,5 km 1.2
12.10: Sluitingsprijs Putte-Kapelle -Bel- 1.3
Max van Heeswijk (Ned-Usp)

13.10: Milano-Torino -Ita- 199 km 1.1
Marcos Serrano Rodriguez (Spa-Lst)

14.10: Giro del Piemonte -Ita- 186 km 1.1
Allan Davis (Aus-Lst)

17.10: Chrono des Herbiers (Time Trial) -Fra- 48,15 km 1.3
Bert Roesems (Bel-Reb)

Yaroslav Popovych, Serhiy Goncha

© 2004 SEP Editrice
Cassina de Pecchi (Milan-Italy)
www.sepeditrice.com
info@sepeditrice.it

Cycling 2004
© 2004 VeloPress®, American edition

Printed in Italy.

10 9 8 7 6 5 4 3 2 1

Distributed in the United States and Canada by Publishers Group West
International Standard Book Number: 1-931382-58-1

VeloPress®
1830 North 55th Street
Boulder, Colorado 80301–2700 USA
303/440-0601 • Fax 303/444-6788 • E-mail velopress@insideinc.com

To purchase additional copies of this book or other VeloPress® books, call 800/234-8356 or visit us on the Web at velopress.com.

PHOTO ROBERTO BETTINI

copyright
www.bettiniphoto.com

SPECIAL THANKS

GianFranco Soncini, Cor Vos, Marketa Navratilova, Hans Roth,
Peter Witek, Lars Roonbog, Antonio Pisoni, Stefano Rellandini.

LAYOUT

Jessica Bono
Thomas LuFont
Drope Yly & Nik
Eurovision

ART DIRECTOR

Alberto Pedrali

TEXTS

Pier Bergonzi

TRANSLATORS

Tim Maloney
Miriam Nordeman
Beate Herberich

PRINT

Poligrafica Antenore
Padova-Italy